DAILY READINGS FROM THE BIBLE

NEW
Daylight

Edited by Shelagh Brown   *May–August 1996*

❯❯The Bible Reading Fellowship

Writers in this issue

Rosemary Green works with Springboard, the Archbishops' Initiative in Evangelism. She is a lay member of the team, and licensed to preach and minister in the Provinces of Canterbury and York. She is the author of *God's Catalyst*; and *Responding to the Holy Spirit* in our audio cassette series 'Draw Near and Listen'.

The Reverend David Winter is a priest in the Hermitage with the Coldash Team Ministry in Berkshire. A regular contributor to *Thought for the Day* and *Prayer for the Day*, he was formerly head of religious broadcasting at the BBC. He is a popular writer, and the author of BRF's best-selling Lent book, *What's in a Word?*

The Reverend Marcus Maxwell is Rector of St John's, Heaton Mersey in Lancashire. Chairman of BRF's Publications Committee, he has been a member of the *New Daylight* team from the start.

The Reverend Henry Wansbrough, OSB, is Principal of St Benet's Hall, Oxford, a writer, a broadcaster and General Editor of The New Jerusalem Bible.

The Reverend Graham Dodds is the Rector of Walcot in Bath and married to Pauline. They met when they were both music students, and they have two children, Helen and Rosie, and two labrador dogs. A regular broadcaster on Radio Bristol, Graham loves music, drama and walking the dogs.

The Reverend Shelagh Brown is Editor of *New Daylight*, a commissioning editor for BRF, a writer, broadcaster and a non-stipendiary minister in Weston-on-the-Green, Oxfordshire.

Profiles of **Adrian Plass** and **The Reverend Canon Douglas Cleverley Ford** are in *The BRF Magazine*.

THE BRF
Magazine

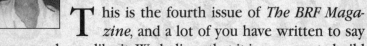

The Editor writes...

This is the fourth issue of *The BRF Magazine*, and a lot of you have written to say how much you like it. We believe that it is one way to build up and strengthen the fellowship side of BRF—to keep you in touch with all that we are doing in different parts of the world, and to update you on news of our team and our writers. This time the writer profiles are double-length: on Canon Douglas Cleverley Ford and Adrian Plass.

The Bishop of Coventry, Simon Barrington-Ward, has taken over the 'Christian Life' piece for the next few issues. This regular feature is here because another purpose of the *Magazine* is to suggest ways which might help you to 'grow in grace and in the knowledge of God'.

'grow in ... the knowledge of God'

We also give you details of our various publications, which have the sole aim of providing you with resources for Bible reading and study (both personal and in groups) and for prayer, Holy Communion and spirituality.

Finally, a personal note, to tell you that in July 1995 I moved from Reigate to Oxford. I can't see the hills from my window any more, or the field of Shetland sheep. But I can see Port Meadow, with cows and horses grazing there, and I know that beyond them is the river. I can't actually see that. Only the boats moving slowly along, and the willow trees that grow on the river bank. So I find myself reflecting on 'the river of the water of life, bright as crystal, flowing from the throne of God and of the Lamb' (Revelation 22:1, NRSV). We can't see that, yet—and John saw it in a symbolic vision. But one day we *shall* see, and be satisfied.

Shelagh Brown

Richard Fisher writes...

T he *BRF Magazine* is a year old! We hope you have enjoyed the articles, news and information included in the last three issues. Thank you for all your letters—it has been great to have so many positive comments. One lady wrote: 'I want to congratulate you on your "magazine" section—full of *personal* interest. It makes you all come alive for us!'

New columnists

In this issue we introduce two new regular columnists: The Rt Revd Simon Barrington-Ward, Bishop of Coventry, takes over from Shelagh Brown to write on *The Christian Life*, and Canon Joy Tetley begins a new column *The Vision of God*. Alongside the regular columns you will also find extracts from two new BRF books in our 'Prayer and Reflection' range, *Spirit Borne* and *Heartfelt*.

Why not pay a visit to your local Christian bookshop and have a look at what they have to offer?

tell you about some of these resources, with an order form included so you can order them if you wish. Of course, these are all available from your local Christian bookshop, where you should be able to find the entire range of BRF publications. Why not pay a visit to your local Christian bookshop and take a look at what they have to offer? Their role and ministry is so important and deserves support.

Christian bookshops

BRF publishes books and audio tapes in addition to Bible reading notes and we use the *Magazine* to

Congratulations

Although by the time you read this he will already have been consecrated and taken up his new post,

5

we should like to congratulate John Went on his appointment as Bishop of Tewkesbury in the Gloucester Diocese. John has been a member of the BRF Council since 1990 and is Chairman of the Executive Committee.

Service

Next year is BRF's 75th anniversary. Plans are progressing well for the events and activities which will take place during the year. One firm date for your diary is Thursday 30 January 1997 when there will be a Service of Thanksgiving and Rededication in Westminster Abbey at 12 noon. Tickets are available for this service on a 'first come, first served' basis (see page 160 for details), and we hope that as many of you as possible will be able to join us

a Service of Thanksgiving and Rededication in Westminster Abbey

for what will be a very special occasion.

BRF Prayer

Many of you are familiar with the BRF Prayer which appears regularly in the notes (below). As part of our planning for our 75th anniversary, we would like to invite you to write your own special BRF prayer and send it to us.

We hope to use some of these new prayers during the course of the year of celebration, and may possibly include them in future BRF publications.

P.S. We'll be at the National Christian Resources Exhibition at Sandown Park, Esher once again on 21–24 May 1996. Do come and see us on the BRF stand if you can.

BRF Prayer

*O God our Father, in the holy scripture
you have given us your word to be our teacher and guide:
help us and all the members of our Fellowship
to seek in our reading the guidance of the Holy Spirit,
that we may learn more of you and of your will for us,
and so grow in likeness to your Son, Jesus Christ our Lord.*

Special Projects News

First of all, a big thank you to all of you who are so generously supporting the work of BRF's Special Projects Fund. We have been greatly encouraged also by the many letters of support for our involvement in these particular projects.

For those of you new to BRF, the Special Projects Fund is entirely supported by donations and legacies and is used to finance charitable projects which fall within BRF's remit of providing Bible reading materials. These projects may be on-going or 'one-off' and may be in the UK or overseas.

Current on-going projects include the provision of:

- *New Daylight* on cassette tape at a subsidised rate for those who are formally registered blind

- the large print edition of *New Daylight* at a subsidised rate (to ensure it remains affordable for those with failing sight)

- financial support for a regular Romanian edition of daily Bible reading notes

Having successfully produced three six month volumes of daily Bible reading notes based on the model of *New Daylight* with a printed Bible passage (from the Romanian Cornilescu translation), comment and prayer, our Romanian partner is now producing an annual one year volume. BRF is supporting some 40% of the total costs (approximately $5,000).

In addition we have recently sent funds to the Anglican province of Myanmar (formerly Burma) to enable them to incorporate a Bible reading plan into their diocesan newsletter, and we have supplied quantities of *Kriss Akabusi on track with the Bible* and *Inside Stories* for use in outreach in prisons.

We are always looking out for potential new special projects, so if you know of a particular cause or project that fits within BRF's remit, and which you think may be if interest, please do write and tell us.

Focus Spot

A t the beginning of 1995 Mum died from cancer. Those months were deeply painful and perplexing for both of us, and have left scars. My greatest need has been to learn how to be still before God—to be in his presence and receive the warmth of his healing love. But I am not very good at being still.

When I look back at difficult moments in my life I can see, with hindsight, that they are often times of growth and learning. We have recently published *Spirit Borne*, a small book about biblical meditation—not a discipline I know. But I suspect that it may become a new avenue of prayer for me—helping me to find that peace and quiet strength for which I long. *Spirit Borne* encourages us to use scripture to still us in the presence of God, to dwell on the Bible's positive and affirming statements about God and his Son Jesus, and to let them sink in deep. It's so easy to know it in the head but not in the heart. One of the positive memories I have of the months surrounding Mum's death is the comfort I received when we read words of scripture at her funeral.

I find it easiest to pray in the countryside, or in the car when I am driving. For me creation is a tremendous stimulus to prayer and reflection. But, as Shelagh Brown points out in *Feeding on God*, you can discover God through all of life—if you know where to look. William Sykes similarly discovered traces of God everywhere. A priest who lost his faith, he decided to search for evidence of God in the world. In his quest he read widely and was not disappointed. His topical anthologies, the *Visions of...* series, reveal aspects of God in over 2,000 years of Christian and religious experience, across many different disciplines. These are not books you read in one sitting. Bill uses them in his reflection groups with university students, and they are a treasure trove of quotes and ideas for sermons and talks.

I wonder if you have ever known that sense of God seeming remote, or having lost your 'first love for Jesus'. There are times when it can seem as if we are just going through the motions of our faith. What is it that melts the ice and warms our hearts? Perhaps sometimes it's a sermon, or a book that speaks into our situation. Perhaps it's a song which echoes our very thoughts. I have a hunch that *Heartfelt*, by Gerrit Scott Dawson is going to affect people like that. It looks at ten stories of Jesus, and invites you to picture yourself in them.

Many of the pilgrims that have travelled with us to the Holy Land on our annual pilgrimage have come back with a renewed love for Jesus. In the Church of the Annunciation in Nazareth there is a small simple stained glass window which spoke to me of Christ's love being poured out. If you, like me, are moved to prayer through art, you might like to know that the Bishop of Oxford has written a superb book helping us to reflect on the mystery of God incarnate through art and artefacts. In *A Gallery of Reflections: the Nativity of Christ* Bishop Richard Harries

been praying all their lives, to deepen their prayer relationship with God. I gather some have been using it in groups.

I have friends I see often and friends I don't see for months on end— yet we seem to be able to pick up just where we left off when we last spoke. There have been times in my life when my prayer relationship with God has been more like the latter— but I know I have been the loser— there is a lot of truth in that telling old slogan 'seven days without prayer makes one weak!'.

Jackie Vincent

introduces us to paintings and artefacts which depict the Christmas story, from the annunciation through to the presentation of Christ in the temple, expertly drawing out both their historical and spiritual significance.

Some of you have commented on how much you have enjoyed Joyce Huggett's books. Her *Learning the Language of Prayer* was designed to help individuals, both beginners and those who have

'seven days without prayer makes one weak!'

PS If you ever have to open or close groups or meetings in prayer, you might be interested to know of our *Prayer Cards*. They are based on five seasons in the church year and provide prayers from around the world, Bible readings and responses for corporate use. Their purpose is to keep prayer at the centre of this Decade of Evangelism as the millennium approaches.

To order copies of these titles, contact your local Christian bookshop or use the order form on page 31.

The Christian Life

Simon Barrington-Ward

Simon Barrington-Ward is the Bishop of Coventry, and for the next few issues of *The BRF Magazine* he will take over our regular feature on *The Christian Life*. In future he will *write* the articles, but for this one, Shelagh Brown put two crucial questions to him.

If someone wants to grow, and to deepen their relationship with God, what can they do?

I believe that the first thing is to look back into your own life and think over those moments of forgiveness that you have experienced. For me all the growth points have come out of forgiveness. Points of forgiveness and points of healing where I have learned something through the pain and the change.

So it is good to be very quietly still and to think over those things. But then, very soon, I think you need to have a group to belong to. I am not sure that I can separate sitting by yourself and opening yourself to the love and forgiveness of God from being in a group which is beginning to share (rather nervously at first but gradually getting braver) the points at which you and other people have experienced forgiveness.

That might not be the starting point for everyone in the group. Some people might want to talk more broadly about some experience they have had of God, and I don't think that matters. I picked on forgiveness because it is often a point that reveals not only our weaknesses and our needs but also the way in which we don't have to be afraid. We can grow out of being vulnerable, and out of the very things which seem painful and bad. We begin to embrace them and to see that out of those things good can come.

> *We can grow out of being vulnerable, and out of the very things which seem painful and bad.*

That goes with a Bible study where you could explore together how a particular passage illuminated what you had just been talking about. That will take you deeper into a realization of the actual reality between you and each other and so between you and God.

I tried to help our children to learn about forgiveness very early on, and I realized that the most effective (and painful) way of teaching them was having to repent and ask their forgiveness myself. But it gradually became a reality for them, and it helped me. And it's something that is constantly happening.

If I get into some difficulty with someone—perhaps in the diocese— and I realize that I've got to go and talk this thing out with them, I've got to be able to acknowledge where I'm wrong and say that I'm sorry. Not to overdo it, but to take the real thing that's painful and to deal with it. There can be a tremendous growth through that for both of us, and that sort of experience is one of the great growth points into a deepening awareness of God.

Alongside forgiveness there is the parallel theme of thankfulness—the deep thankfulness—which is so enormously important. What are those good memories that you look back to? What are the areas where you have experienced something of the fulness and the richness of God?

What are the areas where you have experienced something of the fulness and the richness of God?

Once when I was small I went into a wood and I put my hand on a tree and looked across the wood. I don't think I'd ever seen a bluebell wood before. There were rows of bluebells, and I remember seeing the incredible wave after wave of them going away, and the shape of people moving amongst them. The whole thing suddenly became one. I was holding on to the tree and I remember that I was part of the tree and it was part of me. And everything was one and everything was whole. Then a voice was calling my name and I was like someone coming up to the surface from some deep ocean. It had gone, and I was back with other things. But I never forgot it.

So speak to other people about some of the moments where (perhaps in small ways) things really gave you a deep sense of wonder of joy of richness. People come out with all sorts of things in a group. But it's good too to do that sort of thing by oneself. Just opening up before God about what the things are that he has touched you through. The sense of wonder—like the breath of God entering into you.

It seems to me that those two things—forgiveness and thankfulness— flow together into and out of the Bible study and into and out of the prayer. So that our prayer is be one of profound thanksgiving, profound longing and yearning.

In this diocese I have tried to encourage parishes to form groups. I have urged them to develop the idea of putting right our relationships both with one another and with God. Putting our relationships right with one another means beginning to see very clearly the ways in which we are failing other parts of the diocese. Perhaps the way the better off parts of the diocese are failing the poor parts or the suffering parts. To realize where we are not weeping with those who weep as well as rejoicing with those who rejoice.

We also have to recognize the ways in which we go along in a rut in our own parish, and have cliques and different relationships which are against each other. The way forward isn't to sit in our group and decide how other people must put this right. It's to do what we can do to help to deepen these relationships, so as to bring about reconciliation. There will be a sense of brokeness and forgiveness, and then there will be a turning towards each other and discovering a deeper trust and a deeper relationship—in which we are able to acknowledge and accept each other more profoundly in God and in which we experience his acceptance and love through each other.

If that spreads we shall have a culture of forgiveness in the church in which it is all right to be a sinner and to have failed and to have made a mistake. And even all right to have offended someone. Because through those things we can break through to something deeper.

If someone is overwhelmed by the pain and need of the world, and they feel they are facing five thousand hungry people and they've only got two little fishes and five small rolls, what on earth can they do?

This is very, very difficult and very, very painful, and I think that the only thing one can do is through a twofold movement of action and prayer. To try to join in as far as you can in your own prayer with that constant yearning and longing of God for the world.

I have used the Jesus Prayer—and I have helped people to learn just what I have been talking about through it. Because I have found that when the Jesus Prayer is prayed deeply you have a sense both of the joy that we have been talking about and of the wonder of God. As you say the words 'Lord Jesus Christ, Son of God' (and almost think 'Lord Jesus Christ, Love of God') you are as it were entering into the presence, and you have this tremendous sense of joy. Then the very presence, the very joy and the very wonder of the sense of the presence of God sets going a yearning, a longing... 'Have mercy on me...' And it's not only 'Have mercy on *me*' but—as they sometimes say in the monasteries—it's 'Have mercy on me and on your world'

That yearning and longing for the world to be different is in the heart of God. The whole creation is groaning and the Spirit himself is groaning and travailing with it, and we ourselves have this groaning and travailing within ourselves. There is a deep longing and yearning in God which we can tune into and in which we share.

As we respond to that in prayer we can ask for wisdom to see what particular bit of this enormous web of suffering we can touch on, and to know where we can make our contribution. There will be a particular thing, and we want not only to be giving, praying, informing ourselves, and visiting, but also getting involved in some small part of that which will be a little sign or token of the whole, and to be working for that. We shall start to become much more sensitized to things.

People here in the parishes have sometimes had the same sort of experience: perhaps when they have been to visit some other part of the diocese where people are much more deprived or where they are struggling; or else when they just go to visit a friend in hospital. They suddenly see the depths of all sorts of needs and sufferings about which they had never known. They are made more aware of it and they become more sensitive. Then they begin to join in the yearning both in their prayer and in some action of loving and serving that they take, which is given to them.

This may sound rather general, but once you give yourself to this movement you will find that particular things start opening up for you. God is summoning you just to take a step...

The Vision of God: part 1

Joy Tetley

A snatch of dialogue overheard on a railway station: 'When do *you* think things are going to get better?' 'God knows,' came the reply.

The name of God, it seems, is common currency in our verbal culture and exchange. We hear it all the time. But *is* God more than an expletive? Does our continuing conversational invocation of God betoken some kind of hidden yearning—some inner longing for a Being who, in some sense, *will* make things better—or is God just a conveniently expressive word?

Theologically speaking, it has to be said that God is traditionally believed to constitute a very expressive word indeed. The writers of Judaeo-Christian scriptures certainly had a profound and motivating conviction of both the reality and the active presence of God. Theirs was a God who spoke, who communicated, who engaged in dialogue, who entered into human experience. Theirs was a God whose word was creative, powerful, challenging, enriching, inviting, loving, questioning, healing. The language and imagery they used to give voice to their conviction was deeply meaningful to themselves and their first audience. I want to suggest that the essence of what the biblical writers were trying to communicate is still crucially important in our day and age—that the God they believed in and proclaimed *is real* and can still touch and change our lives for good.

To explore that claim, let's begin by focusing on a key passage from the New Testament: Hebrews 4:12–16. Here in these verses is something of a nutshell summary of the heart of the writer's message. Hebrews, incidentally, is not so much

> *Theirs was a God who spoke, who communicated, who engaged in dialogue, who entered into human experience.*

15

an epistle as an impassioned and carefully argued sermon. It was designed to get through to a community in crisis, a community tempted to give up. It therefore deals with the fundamentals of faith.

Verses 12–16 present a graphic picture of what the writer sees as the reality of our human condition in the context of God. Total exposure. Terrifying thought. Here, the author of Hebrews uses language that clearly alludes to the first Adam and Eve, whose story we read in Genesis 2 and 3. The naked Adam and Eve, archetypal human beings, discovered after eating forbidden fruit that they could not hide from God. God's searching voice exposed them completely, both outwardly and inwardly. God penetrated their hiding place and their excuses.

So it is still with humankind (says the preacher). We are utterly laid bare before God who made us. We can cover up nothing, including those aspects of our being that we're reluctant to admit—even to ourselves. We are totally open and totally accountable to the God whose penetrating word pierces to the heart of our vulnerable nakedness. We have to confront the truth about ourselves. There is nowhere to hide.

This is not a comfortable state of affairs. But, then, the whole history of the people of God would seem to suggest that even *their* primary vocation is not to an easy, undisturbed life. Certainly the witness of the Scriptures is that God seems painfully prone to questioning, prodding and unsettling the community of faith, saying again and again in various ways, 'Where are you?' They can murmur and complain as much as they like, God is not about to give up the struggle. The people of God need constantly moving on from where they are—in every sense of that phrase. As the writer of Hebrews puts it elsewhere, 'Here we have no abiding city'. There is no earthly place of security to which we can lay permanent claim, in which we can hide.

Is God a sadist, then—this God before whom we have no protection? That's a crucial question. It has to be addressed. For many, at least in their heart of hearts, the answer to the question (an answer born of bitter experience) is 'yes'. God the sadist

We have to confront the truth about ourselves.

seems to have wielded the sword to devastating effect.

The preacher who produced Hebrews points us, as ever, to a liberating way through. He goes on to stress a further truth—a truth almost beyond belief, yet profoundly real, a truth that pulsates at the heart of the Gospel. If we are laid bare before God, God lays himself bare before us. God's response to our inherent weakness and failure and fear is not to condemn or destroy. God's response to human suffering is not malicious delight or unfeeling withdrawal. In Jesus, ultimate divine self-expression, God experiences at first hand what it means to be human in a less than perfect world. In Jesus, God becomes like us in every respect. In the fullest and most literal sense, God knows!

It is not just that God knows all about us. In Jesus, God knows from the inside the force of our human condition, with all its potential for glory and for shame. On every level, physical, emotional, spiritual, Jesus knows what it's like to live humanly—and to suffer.

This is the God before whom we are exposed. This is the God to whom we are invited to draw near: not in grovelling fear but in bold confidence and in total honesty, sure of insider understanding and a loving welcome. There is no appointment system. We can approach whenever we like. And there are no intermediaries to negotiate. Our right of access is as direct as it is continuous. At God's throne of grace we can lay down the burden of pretence. We are free to be ourselves. At God's throne of grace we can lay down the burden of our fears and uncertainties, of our own suffering and that of others. At God's throne of grace we can be immersed in that mercy and grace which, again and again, is the re-making and the re-clothing of us. Here, things can be 'made better'. Here is our ultimate and unfailing security.

Our right of access is as direct as it is continuous.

Joy Tetley is Principal of the East Anglian Ministerial Training Course and specializes in the areas of ministry and biblical studies. She is author of Sunday by Sunday— *commentaries and prayers which follow the readings in the Anglican lectionary.*

Profile: Adrian Plass

Adrian Plass is a best-selling author, and his best-known title, *The Sacred Diary of Adrian Plass aged 37 ¾*, has sold half a million copies worldwide.

He is in great demand internationally as a speaker, and when he spoke to me on the phone to tell me a bit about his life story for this profile he had just got back from three weeks in South Africa. He has been to Australia and New Zealand, and is a regular speaker at Spring Harvest and Greenbelt. Adrian Plass is very successful. But it hasn't always been like that—and life has been very tough.

'As a boy I had a very tense childhood,' he told me. 'There was a lot of conflict at home, and a lot of tension between my parents. There was lot of untidiness in my life, which made school difficult.'

I wasn't quite sure what he meant by that, so he explained. 'Things like being academically quite positive and well inclined at secondary school—but the general feeling of chaos at home meant my homework hardly ever got done. And gradually I slid down to the pit of the D stream.'

He felt desperate, and escaped into a fantasy world. 'I imagined a

future as a film star', he said, 'and I lived in my own little world. I truanted a lot, and at the age of fifteen I was expelled.'

After that he went to a further education college and did a foundation course in drama. 'By the skin of my teeth I ended up with an A level and a couple of O levels. Then I trained to be an actor.' At drama school he met Bridget, and they fell in love and decided to get married. They have been married now for twenty-five years, and have four children: Matthew (21), Joe (16), David (15) and Katie (8).

'But we gave up the idea of acting,' he told me, 'because we didn't think that marriage and the theatre would have worked for us.' He trained as a teacher, and Bridget and he took on a residential job and worked with children in care. He tells the story of that time in their life in *Broken Windows, Broken Lives*.

It was very tough, and in 1984 Adrian had a stress illness. 'That's when the writing started,' he said, 'as a sort of therapy. I'd already started doing a late night TV programme called *Company*. and Bridget was on it as well. Then a publisher asked me to write a book, and Andy Butcher, the editor of *Family* magazine, wrote to me at the same time and asked me to do a column called *The Secret Diary of Adrian Plass*.'

He started to write the column, and it was an immediate success. 'It was very useful for me,' he said, 'because it was a reasonably constructive way of expressing some of the hurt and anger I felt about the church in general.'

Then the same publisher for whom he had done his book *Join The Company* asked him to turn the columns into a book. 'And by then,' he said, 'I had already started reading them aloud at places like Spring Harvest. That was before the book came out. And when it did it just exploded.'

Adrian has a brilliant sense of humour, and I wondered if it was ever a strain when people had such a high expectation of being made to laugh. 'I enjoy amusing people,' he told me, 'and it's great fun doing it. But people don't always recognise that my intention is deadly serious— and it always has been. But sometimes the weight of expectation is difficult.

'It's like a child who comes along in the middle of the night and says, "I am hungry"—and he really means "I'm frightened." A wise person will know that, and go and turn his light on.'

I wasn't sure who was who in Adrian's illustration, so I asked him. He laughed, a bit ruefully. 'Oh,' he said, 'I am the one who needs the light on!

Books by Adrian Plass

Broken Windows Broken Lives
The Sacred Diary of Adrian Plass
 Aged 37 3/4
The Final Boundary
The Growing Pains of Adrian Plass
 (previously published as *Join The Company*)
Clearing Away the Rubbish
The Horizontal Epistles of
 Andromeda Veal
A Smile on the Face of God
The Theological Tapes of Leonard
 Thynne
Cabbages for the King
The Unlocking
An Alien at St Wilfreds
Stress Family Robinson
You say Tomato

And, by the time this goes to print, a book will just have been published, called *The Sacred Diary of Adrian Plass, Christian Speaker, Aged 45 3/4*.

Profile: Douglas Cleverley Ford

T he Reverend Canon Douglas Cleverley Ford was born in Sheringham, Norfolk. He went to Great Yarmouth Grammar School and then to the London College of Divinity in the University of London. After graduation he stayed on as a theological tutor, and it was during that time that he met and fell in love with a young woman called Olga.

'I was helping on an evangelistic campaign in the Midlands,' he told me, 'and the Inter Varsity Fellowship, who were running it, made an appeal to anyone who could put up students. I went to stay with a couple, in a very comfortable house, and one day my hostess said to me "I would like you to meet a friend of mine— she's very elegant." And she was!

'We sat next to each other on the sofa, and she asked me how I interpreted a verse in the first chapter of John's Gospel. "Well, well!" I thought, she doesn't look this sort at all. She must be a Christian.

'She had a flat in London, and we used to meet there. And after two years we married. I believe in providence. She has been the support and stay of my whole ministry.

' "You're too booky!" she said to me. "You ought to get out from your theological lectureship and meet ordinary people. You'd be much better." And I did. I would have had to anyway, because there was no room for a married man on the staff. But that was the making of me. I got out among people. And she supported me all the 54 years that we were married.'

'She died in October, 1993, and I found her in the hall. It was my turn to cook the lunch—and I rang the gong. She was always so punctual that when she didn't come I went to look for her. I went into the corridor, and there she was on the floor. She'd died with the Hoover in her hand doing the floor. She lived right up to the last, and I miss her.'

I asked Douglas Cleverley Ford to tell me how he had got involved with the College of Preachers. 'I was asked to go on a small committee led by Archbishop Coggan,' he told me, 'though he was then the Bishop of Bradford. We went away for three days to discuss the lamentable state of preaching in the Church of England and to think what we could do about it, and we came up with this idea of a college of preachers. We had nothing. No money. No base. No building. No plans. And they asked me to be the first director. So I began to run residential courses for clergy in various centres. And the extraordinary thing was that it exceeded all our expectatons. It grew very rapidly, and after thirteen years it had 2,000 members.'

'Then I went to be Chaplain to the Archibishop of Canterbury at Lambeth Palace—for nearly six years with Archbishop Donald Coggan, then for nine months with Archbishop Robert Runcie.'

Douglas Cleverley Ford has written 36 books, and because of his skills in writing and preaching I asked him for some advice on both. He was quite clear about it. 'People want to know about people and about events,' he told me. 'It's no good writing about theories or doctrines. It's not that they aren't important, but they are on the margin. People's interest is in people, and in things that have happened. This is the way a good deal of the Bible is written, and if you stray from this then you stray from the basics.'

But it isn't only in preaching and writing that Canon Cleverley Ford is an expert. 'I'm quite a practical person', he told me 'I can do anything in the house. I'm a DIY person. I paint the house, and I do the washing, and I can cook. I love gardening, and I enjoy listening to classical music. I don't play any instruments, but I was in a choir all my life ever since I was seven years old.'

As readers of *New Daylight* will know, he loves to sing the psalms out loud—and recommends that his readers should do the same if they can possibly manage it. Whatever it sounds like— because God hears the music of the heart, even when the outward sound isn't all that it might be.

People's interest is in people

Day by Day with the Psalms *is a selection of Douglas Cleverley Ford's notes on the Psalms from* New Daylight. *Now available from your local Christian bookshop, or see order form, page 31.*

An extract from
Spirit Borne

An introduction to biblical meditation
by Paul Bunday

When the business world starts promoting a spiritual technique there must be money in it. And meditation is a money-spinner these days because so many firms have found that working hours are lost through stress-related illnesses.

Management feels that any technique which produces results can be used to prevent profits falling too sharply. Of course, some of these practices are far from Christian and so, in the long run, may produce more problems than they solve...

...It was only about five years ago when my parochial ministry was passing through a period of frustration that I began to harness the practice of meditation more deeply into daily devotional life.

I believe that there are three vital reasons for developing the practice of meditation. The first is pre-eminent and the other two come equal second.

The first reason for engaging in meditation is that it focuses on the glory of God: it gives us a vision of his transcendence and immanence, which enables us to appreciate the reality of his nearness. He is the almighty, holy, living Lord. In meditation we give him our full attention, and we do it quietly, holding ourselves still, looking at him trustfully, reverently, knowing that he is looking at us compassionately. Everything else in life recedes. We are actually obeying the first commandment which is to hallow God's holy name. God, himself, is our central point of focus.

Almost certainly the act of meditation has begun with the sense of God there and I myself here. But it now needs to develop into something more profound. 'God-there' and 'I-here' needs to progress to the intimacy of 'I-Thou' which is the expression of true relationship.

Secondly, we affirm that meditation is a deeply healing experience, as many are discovering. Hence the interest of the commercial world. The whole of the human personality is involved. Because we have decided that it is important, or at least worth a try, we 'will' to engage in it, and so we make time and opportunity to practise it either by ourselves or in a group—ideally both. Our mind is involved because we hold, quietly and rationally, some particular word of truth in our thoughts. Here words of Scripture are of the utmost importance so that we can ensure that it is God's truth that we are inwardly digesting. Our emotions are also involved although not self-stimulated. In the quietness of the meditation emotion may well be released because we are allowing the truth of God, focussed in a prayer-phrase, to drop through our conscious minds down into our subconscious. Normally this will produce a sense of peace and well-being, a release of tension and stress and may finally evolve into an experience of wholeness, or even holiness which, of course, are inter-connected. God, the Holy Spirit, is touching us in body, mind and spirit therefore wholeness should be the natural result. We do not even need to ask for it for, by obeying spiritual law, it should inevitably come.

Thirdly, and equally important with the healing aspect of meditation, is the value that it has in making great Christian truths more personal, more part of us. Great preaching can do this but in a different way. The words of truth spoken by the preacher coupled with his own conviction and emotion can grip us in such a way that we enter into a new depth of understanding. However, in meditation we take great Christian truths and by revolving them around in our minds, chewing the cud on them as it were, we allow them to become more and more part of our experience—but this is done quietly with the body and emotions held as still as possible. It is certainly not mindless repetition in the hope that one day we shall really start believing what we are saying. Rather, it is taking a prayer phrase which we have received at an initial level of faith and, by warm welcome and quiet repetition, allowing the Holy Spirit to lead us to a deeper level of understanding. In this sense meditation is the process by which we give the Holy Spirit space to deepen his influence in our lives and to reprogramme our minds.

It is important to set out the truly objective facts about meditation as so many people have the idea that it's a pious, subjective exercise that inadequate people undertake as an escape from reality. It is quite the reverse. It brings the glorious, transcendent reality of God into our experience in a remarkable way. It is a spiritual exercise that can benefit all Christians and it may well be especially powerful for the many people today who are subject to stress. It also helps us to overcome the perennial problem of translating head knowledge into heart knowledge, of transforming the purely cerebral into the warmth of personal experience. As the classic devotional writers tell us, it enables us to possess our possessions in Christ and to become what we already truly are in him.

Spirit Borne offers insights and advice to provide a practical introduction to biblical meditation. Three sections of actual meditations are also included: Meditations focussed on the Worship of God, Meditations on Healing and Wholeness, and Meditations that deepen Faith and Experience.

Lord Coggan has written of *Spirit Borne*:

The strength of this little book is that it does not emerge from a cloistered cell or an academic study, but from the pen of a man who has spent his ministry of nearly forty years in busy parishes. He has given us a spiritual book—well earthed.

To obtain a copy of *Spirit Borne*, contact your local Christian bookshop or use the order form on page 31.

An extract from
Heartfelt

Finding our way back to God
by Gerrit Scott Dawson

The author writes in his introduction: 'This book is for people who are looking for a stronger connection with God. I have in mind those who are familiar with Christianity but who feel that their experience of traditional faith has not been enough for them. Perhaps a fresh approach to relating to Jesus as we find him in the Gospels would be helpful. If we could tunnel under the wall which has blocked us from God, we might be able to open the channel for a vital spiritual energy to flow into our lives . . .

'. . . I believe passionately that such a relationship can be developed as we meet Jesus in the Gospels. I invite you to "try on" the idea that Jesus still speaks, still lives, still engages people who encounter him. Working with this assumption, if only imaginatively, we will explore such questions as: What does Jesus offer? What does he want from me? What will happen if I follow him?

'We will be working with ten stories of Jesus. My hope is that you will be able to find yourself in the characters of these narratives. If we can hook up our lives with their lives for a while, it just might be possible that we can be moved, healed, transformed, and invigorated as they were.'

The following extract is taken from the chapter 'Watching Down the Foreign Road' which considers the story of the Prodigal Son (Luke 15:11–24):

To know that someone waits

What would it mean to learn that someone is watching with straining eyes down the road to catch a glimpse of you? When we are far from home, what would happen if we realized that someone was waiting for the first signs of our return from a foreign land, waiting to celebrate our first steps home with open arms and a banquet of celebration?

In the epilogue of Dostoyevsky's novel, *Crime and Punishment*, we read of the beginning of renewal for the story's main character, Raskolnikov. Towards the beginning of the story, Raskolnikov had murdered an old woman pawnbroker, feeling no remorse and justifying his act as ridding society of an undesirable. Throughout the epic, he was wholly absorbed in himself—a narcissist fit for the twentieth century.

Though Raskolnikov is certainly an unattractive character, one woman loved him all along. Sonia even followed Raskolnikov all the way to the Siberian work camp where he was sentenced to seven years of hard labour for his crime. She came to the fence every day to speak with him during their brief breaks in the work.

For a long time Raskolnikov spurned her presence. It meant nothing to him. He would remain quiet when he was with her, as if annoyed. Then Raskolnikov fell ill and was placed in the hospital ward for many weeks.

Our shame will not be recrimination, but with

Sonia tried to see him but only rarely could gain admittance. Still, she came every day, 'sometimes only to stand a minute and look up at the windows of the ward.'

Raskolnikov's condition improved slowly. One evening he felt strong enough to rise from his bed and go to the window. He looked out and saw Sonia standing at the hospital gate; she appeared to be waiting for something. 'Something stabbed him to the heart at that minute.' He realised that every day he had been ill, unable to rise, believing himself to be alone in his misery, Sonia had come to the gate to wait awhile for him.

Raskolnikov looked for Sonia eagerly the next day. But she did not come. Nor the next day. And then Raskolnikov understood that he was waiting for Sonia. Before, Sonia had been the one waiting; now he was waiting for Sonia. Before it had made no difference to him, but now he was expecting her. Before he loathed her; now he discovered that as he waited for her, he loved her.

When they met again at last, Raskolnikov found that 'all at once something seemed to seize him and fling him at her feet. He wept and threw his arms around her knees.' Sonia had outwaited his self- absorption until love broke through him at last. The one so far from home, in Siberia and detached from his own soul, finally understood that someone had waited for him every day. He reconnected to life and came home to himself.

There is one who waits for us. He stands everyday in the yard looking up at the ward where we lie on a bed, mired in thoughts of our condition. He comes every day and stands in the cold winter night, and he waits while we think life is only this sick bed and the wants of our illness. He waits in the yard for the evening we get up and look out the window and see him there, and our hearts are stabbed. Someone is waiting for me to come home! Our shame will not be answered with recrimination, but with tenderness, forgiveness. He has not waited begrudgingly; he is not angry. This loving one has let go all the time that has gone by. He just wants us in his arms.

The father strained his eyes down the foreign road for any sign of his son. The boy didn't know that, of course. He didn't really think of his father until he was so hungry that pride was impossible. Then he got up and started home.

We can wait that long if we like. The trouble is we may not get so abjectly hungry that we have no choice until many years have passed. But if we were to step into this story Jesus told and begin to consider that the father is waiting for us now, would that be enough to get us to our feet?

We may be able to slop the pigs for a long time, if we do not believe there is any other choice, if shame prevents thoughts of home. But what yearning homeward is awakened when we discover that there is one who waits for us, watching every day for any sign of our return, ready to embrace us even in our filth, to love us through the shame!

George Herbert concluded his poem of rebellion with these words,

> But as I raved and grew more fierce and wild
> At every word,
> Methought I heard one calling, *Child!*
> And I replied, *My Lord*.

There are so many of us who feel as if we are far away from something we need to be close to. The emotion is very nebulous. And often if someone tries to diagnose us with precision, to say, 'What you need is . . .' we close it off. What we are missing is so important to us that instinctively we close out superficial explanations. We have come to ourselves enough to know that we need to start toward home. But we may not be sure in which direction to begin. We may not be at all convinced anyone will welcome us when we arrive. The rest of this book is for those who feel the urge to get up and start down the road towards home . . .

To obtain a copy of *Heartfelt*, contact your local Christian bookshop or use the order form on page 31.

SPREAD THE WORD

Among a number of discoveries made in a nationwide MORI poll commissioned by BBC1's *Songs of Praise*, the following was revealed: 'Churchgoers were also found to take a traditional approach to religious practice, with more than 80% praying more than once a week and 67% praying every day. Bible-reading proved less common, with only 44% reading the Bible more than once a week and only 26% reading it daily. A total of 12% said they never read it.'

Anecdotal evidence from our own readers suggests that the majority encountered BRF Bible reading notes for the first time when introduced to them by a member of their church or family, or by a friend.

So why not help us to spread the word, and give a Gift Subscription to a friend or a member of your family? To do this, just fill in the coupon below (please ensure that you complete both sides of the coupon) and send it to BRF.

Please send the Gift Subscription to:

Name _____

Address _____

_____

_____ Postcode _____

Please send to the above, beginning with the May/Sep 1996 issue (delete as appropriate):

	(please tick box)
FIRST LIGHT	☐ £9.00
GUIDELINES	☐ £9.00
NEW DAYLIGHT	☐ £9.00
NEW DAYLIGHT LARGE PRINT	☐ £12.00

(see over for payment details)

All prices are correct at time of going to press, are subject to the prevailing rate of VAT and may be subject to change without prior warning.

ND0296   **The Bible Reading Fellowship is a Registered Charity**

PAYMENT DETAILS

Please complete the payment details below and send your coupon, with appropriate payment, to:

The Bible Reading Fellowship
Peter's Way
Sandy Lane West
Oxford OX4 5HG

Your Name_____

Your Address_____

_____

_____ Postcode _____

Total enclosed £ _____ (Cheques should be payable to 'BRF')

Payment by Cheque☐ Postal Order☐ Visa☐ Mastercard☐

Card number: ☐☐☐☐ ☐☐☐☐ ☐☐☐☐ ☐☐☐☐

Expiry date of card: ☐☐☐☐

Signature (essential if paying by credit card)_____

   NB: BRF notes are also available from your local Christian bookshop.

The Bible Reading Fellowship is a Registered Charity

ORDER FORM

Please ensure that you complete and send off both pages of this order form.

Please send me the following book(s):

	Quantity	Price	Total
Spirit Borne	_____	£2.99	_____
Feeding On God	_____	£2.99	_____
Visions of Love	_____	£9.99	_____
Visions of Hope	_____	£9.99	_____
Visions of Glory	_____	£9.99	_____
Visions of Faith	_____	£10.99	_____
Heartfelt	_____	£3.99	_____
A Gallery of Reflections: the Nativity of Christ	_____	£9.99	_____
Learning the Language of Prayer (paperback)	_____	£6.99	_____
Prayer Cards (packs of 10):			
Advent	_____	£4.00	_____
Candlemas to Christmas	_____	£4.00	_____
Lent	_____	£4.00	_____
Easter	_____	£4.00	_____
Ordinary seasons	_____	£4.00	_____
Assorted (2 of each)	_____	£4.00	_____
Sunday by Sunday (ASB year 2)	_____	£9.99	_____
Day by Day Volume 1	_____	£10.99	_____
Day by Day Volume 2	_____	£9.99	_____
Day by Day Volume 3	_____	£10.99	_____
Day by Day with the Psalms	_____	£5.99	_____

POSTAGE AND PACKING CHARGES		
order value	UK	Europe
£6.00 & under	£1.00	£2.00
£6.01–£14.99	£2.50	£3.00
£15.00–£29.99	£3.50	£5.00
£30.00 & over	free	enquire

Total Cost of Books £ _____

Postage and Packing £ _____

TOTAL £ _____

(See over for payment details.)

All prices are correct at time of going to press, are subject to the prevailing rate of VAT and may be subject to change without prior warning.

ND0296   **The Bible Reading Fellowship is a Registered Charity**

PAYMENT DETAILS

Please complete the payment details below and send your coupon, with appropriate payment and completed order form to:

The Bible Reading Fellowship
Peter's Way
Sandy Lane West
Oxford OX4 5HG

Name _____

Address _____

_____

_____ Postcode _____

Total enclosed £ _____ (Cheques should be payable to 'BRF')

Payment by Cheque☐ Postal Order☐ Visa☐ Mastercard☐

Card number: ☐☐☐☐ ☐☐☐☐ ☐☐☐☐ ☐☐☐☐ ☐☐☐☐

Expiry date of card: ☐☐☐☐

Signature (essential if paying by credit card)_____

Alternatively you may wish to order books using the BRF telephone order hotline: 01865 748227

NB: These titles are all also available from your local Christian bookshop.

The Bible Reading Fellowship is a Registered Charity

Joel 1:1–7 (GNB)

Pay attention!

This is the Lord's message to Joel son of Pethuel. Pay attention, you older people; everyone in Judah, listen. Has anything like this ever happened in your time or the time of your ancestors? Tell your children about it; they will tell their children, who in turn will tell the next generation. Swarm after swarm of locusts settled on the crops; what one swarm left, the next swarm devoured. Wake up and weep, you drunkards; cry, you wine drinkers; the grapes for making new wine have been destroyed. An army of locusts has attacked our land; they are powerful and too many to count; their teeth are as sharp as those of a lion. They have destroyed our grapevines and chewed up our fig trees. They have stripped off the bark, till the branches are white.

'Pain is [God's] megaphone to rouse a deaf world,' wrote C.S. Lewis in *The Problem of Pain*, and all the Old Testament prophets would have agreed with him. They all spoke the words of God to the particular situation in their own generation, and because they were words inspired by God they have spoken powerfully to every generation. All suffering is not the direct result of human sin, but much of it is the direct result of human selfishness and greed.

In the Western world we don't suffer from plagues of locusts, but last summer Britain and other parts of Europe suffered from a severe drought. We had plenty of rain in the winter, but we are profligate in our use of water and we waste it. Then the crops fail, and in the winter the price of food goes up. The people who suffer most, as always, are the poor. 'I keep a tight ship,' someone said to me, 'but it isn't easy.' Her husband had lost his job, and the two of them were finding it very hard to cope and to look after their children on her pay. This winter it will get even harder.

Consider

Spend some time considering a situation somewhere in your country, or in our world, where there is severe suffering and hardship for some of the people. Then do what Joel told those people to do: 'Pay attention . . . everyone . . . listen . . .' Wait in silence for a few moments, and ask the living God who spoke through the prophets to speak his word to you.

Joel 1:8–12 (GNB)

Cry for joy

Cry, you people, like a young woman who mourns the death of the man she was going to marry. There is no corn or wine to offer in the Temple; the priests mourn because they have no offerings for the Lord. The fields are bare; the ground mourns because the corn is destroyed, the grapes are dried up, and the olive trees are withered. Grieve, you farmers; cry, you that take care of the vineyards, because the wheat, the barley, yes, all the crops are destroyed. The grapevines and fig trees have withered; all the fruit trees have wilted and died. The joy of the people is gone.

Things have gone wrong for the people of Judah because *they* have gone wrong, and God is calling them to put things right. Calling to them to cry out and to lament, like a young woman whose future husband is dead and whose hope for the future has died with him. The relationship she had with him is no longer there—and neither is the relationship which the people of Judah once had with God. But God isn't dead. He is the living God, and he longs to restore the relationship that he created with them (and every human being in the world) to enjoy. Their present desolation and suffering (and ours) could be the way back to God—if only they will listen to what he is saying through his prophet Joel.

The people have lost the joy that they had. 'The joy of the Lord is your strength,' Isaiah had written, and they knew that. But their joy had been in the wrong things: in their prosperity and—for some—in their drinking. Last week a young man told how he goes out drinking every night. 'I want to enjoy myself while I'm young!' he told me, and since I had only just met him we didn't get involved in a deep conversation. But I hope that one day we shall—and in the meantime I shall give him a copy of the book *Kriss Akabusi on Track with the Bible*, in which Kriss tells how his worldly success just didn't satisfy his heart. It never does and it never can.

As the people look at the dry land and the dying crops they are to consider their own dryness and barrenness, and to realize the cause of it.

Reflect

He satisfies those who are thirsty and fills the hungry with good things.

Psalm 107:9 (GNB)

'I have told you this so that my joy may be in you and that your joy may be complete.'

John 15:11 (GNB)

Joel 1:13–20 (GNB)

Cry for help

Put on sackcloth and weep, you priests who serve at the altar! Go into the Temple and mourn all night! There is no corn or wine to offer your God. Give orders for a fast; call an assembly! Gather the leaders and all the people of Judah into the Temple of the Lord your God and cry out to him. The day of the Lord is near; the day when the Almighty brings destruction. What terror that day will bring! We look on helpless as our crops are destroyed. There is no joy in the Temple of our God. The seeds die in the dry earth. There is no grain to be stored, and so the empty granaries are in ruins. The cattle are bellowing in distress because there is no pasture for them; the flocks of sheep also suffer. I cry out to you, Lord, because the pastures and trees are dried up, as though a fire had burnt them. Even the wild animals cry out to you because the streams have become dry.

Joel was crying out to the Lord because of the dry land and the dying crops, and the creatures were crying out as well. But the people needed to join in the crying and mourning, and to recognize the desolation and dryness of the land as a symbol of their own spiritual desolation. They was nothing they could do to bring the crops and the dying seeds to life again. But there was something they could do to bring renewal and refreshment to their own spiritual dryness. They could fast, and cry out in their helplessness to the supreme helper.

The point of the fasting was to pray. To cry out for help, to remember how God had helped them in the past, and to recollect the loving-kindness and mercy of God. As they fasted and prayed the Lord would break through the barriers that they had put up—and they would know the powerful renewing presence of the living God. Fasting was never an end in itself: always a means to an end—and the end was always an encounter with God that led to obedience.

A way to pray

If you are desolate yourself, remember how God has helped you in the past—and reflect on his loving-kindness. If you want refreshment and renewal God will give it to you—but you may just want your present distress to end. Let the Spirit within you use that distress, or the distress of your country or of a person you know, to lead you to cry out for help.

Joel 2:1–3, 10–11 (GNB)

First the bad news . . .

Blow the trumpet; sound the alarm on Zion, God's sacred hill. Tremble, people of Judah! The day of the Lord is coming soon. It will be a dark and gloomy day, a black and cloudy day. The great army of locusts advances like darkness spreading over the mountains. There has never been anything like it, and there never will be again. Like fire they eat up the plants. In front of them the land is like the Garden of Eden, but behind them it is a barren desert. Nothing escapes them . . . The earth shakes as they advance; the sky trembles. The sun and the moon grow dark, and the stars no longer shine. The Lord thunders commands to his army. The troops that obey him are many and mighty. How terrible is the day of the Lord! Who will survive it?

They must have been shattered by Joel's words: telling them that the terrible army devastating their land was the Lord's army. There is an equally shattering image in the book of Revelation, when John is given a vision of the final judgment. He sees 'one like a son of man' seated on a white cloud, with a crown of gold on his head and a sharp sickle in his hand. 'Use your sickle and reap the harvest,' says an angel, 'because the time has come; the earth is ripe for harvest.' So the Son of man swings his sickle over the earth and the earth is harvested (Revelation 14:14–16, GNB).

The Son of man is also the Son of God, and it is Christ who will be the judge on the last day. What lay ahead in the short term, and the long term, for the people of Judah was judgment, and Joel urges them to let their present distress point them to the final judgment.

One day there will be something far worse than the darkness that came from a plague of locusts blotting out the sun. Those who refuse the love and the forgiveness of God will be thrown 'into the outer darkness'—which is a final exclusion from the presence of God who is the eternal light.

Now the good news . . .

For God so loved the world that he gave his one and only Son, that whoever believes in him shall not perish but have eternal life. For God did not send his Son into the world to condemn the world, but to save the world through him . . . Light has come into the world, but men loved darkness instead of light because their deeds were evil.

John 3:16–17, 19 (NIV)

2 Corinthians 5:1–3 (NIV)

Sunday best

Now we know that if the earthly tent we live in is destroyed, we have a building from God, an eternal house in heaven, not built by human hands. Meanwhile we groan, longing to be clothed with our heavenly dwelling, because when we are clothed, we will not be found naked.

'The Vicar took his clothes off!' That is what an entry reads in the Register of Services in a Dorking church. I'd been asked to give a family talk on putting off the old and putting on the new. My talk involved disrobing myself of my ecclesiastical garments before putting on my favourite 'rainbow' jumper which all curates seemed to have at the time. And so it was that the churchwarden, who got me to 'sign the book' at the end of the service had scribbled his note. I only hope the Archdeacon understood on his next visitation.

There was a time when going to church meant 'Sunday best' clothes. Hats suddenly appeared. Suits, uniforms, best dresses decorated the people like flowers decorating the building. It was a mark of respect, a statement saying, 'I want God to be honoured by my appearance on this, his special day.' Unfortunately for some it was none of that. It was about earning more than him or her and keeping others in their place. It was about hiding behind the façade of respectability.

There's an old Bible nicknamed the 'Breeches Bible' because the transla-tors interpreted Adam and Eve making clothes for themselves as sewing themselves some breeches. But why did that happen? Why did they become embarrassed about their nakedness?

A Christian artist in Bath has just celebrated the nude in an exhibition of her work. As you might imagine it has raised a few eyebrows. Yet isn't the story of Adam and Eve telling us something about what God's clothes are like? Love, joy, righteousness, holiness, and many more spiritual qualities are in our heavenly suitcase. There's not much about actual clothes apart from a few white robes in the final book of the Bible.

As I approach God in a communion service it's like a spiritual stripping away. At the most intimate moment of receiving the bread and wine I feel it's like being given a new set of clothes after I've just stained the old ones. Thank God he's both a launderer and a master tailor.

GD

Joel 2:12–17 (GNB)

Fast and pray

'But even now,' says the Lord, 'repent sincerely and return to me with fasting and weeping and mourning. Let your broken heart show your sorrow; tearing your clothes is not enough.' Come back to the Lord your God. He is kind and full of mercy; he is patient and keeps his promise; he is always ready to forgive and not punish ... Blow the trumpet on Mount Zion; give orders for a fast and call an assembly! Gather the people together; prepare them for a sacred meeting; bring the old people; gather the children and the babies too. Even newly married couples must leave their room and come. The priests, serving the Lord between the altar and the entrance of the Temple, must weep and pray: 'Have pity on your people, Lord. Do not let other nations despise us and mock us by saying, "Where is your God?"'

The outward tearing of their clothes was to be a sign of an inner tearing and brokenness. 'A broken and a contrite heart you will not despise' it says in Psalm 51, and when we come to God in penitence and faith he will always be there for us, with his arms wide open. Like the father of the prodigal son when the son wearily came home again because the party had come to a disastrous end and he was hungry. But when the prodigal got home there was another party, in the father's house and in the father's presence. And the father didn't despise him, he delighted in him.

'He is always ready to forgive and not punish,' Joel had said, and it is what he longs to do. To bless all people with abundant happiness—and when we break his laws we break our own hearts. Not in the brokenness of a godly sorrow that leads us to repentance, but in the wretched self-centred sorrow that goes round in circles and doesn't know what to do to make the pain stop.

But there is something we can do, either over our own personal sin and sadness or over the sin of our nation. We can fast and weep and mourn.

The process has to start with the priests, Joel tells them, and in the theology of the New Testament that means all Chrisians, created in and through Christ to be a royal priesthood.

Pray

Pray in repentance and sorrow for yourself and for your country—for such a change of heart that God will be able to do what he longs to do, and bless rather than punish.

Joel 2:18-22 (GNB)

Really satisfied

Then the Lord showed concern for his land; he had mercy on his people. He answered them: 'Now I am going to give you corn and wine and olive oil, and you will be satisfied. Other nations will no longer despise you. I will remove the locust army that came from the north and will drive some of them into the desert. Their front ranks will be driven into the Dead Sea, their rear ranks into the Mediterranean. Their dead bodies will stink. I will destroy them because of all they have done to you ... Animals, don't be afraid. The pastures are green; the trees bear their fruit, and there are plenty of figs and grapes.'

The Good News Bible translation that we are using says that 'the Lord showed concern for his land'—and the original word for 'showed concern' means jealous, or zealous. And in certain situations jealousy is just the right thing to feel—and it can lead to just the right action. A husband or a wife is right to be jealous if the marriage is under threat from another woman or another man. The prophet Hosea fought for his marriage, and pleaded with his wife in a mixture of anger and heartbroken love: 'I will allure her, and bring her into the wilderness, and speak tenderly to her. And there I will give her her vineyards, and make the Valley of Achor a door of hope' (Hosea 2:14–15, RSV).

When Jesus found the traders in the temple at Jerusalem defiling it with their selling of sacrificial animals he drove them out of the temple in holy anger, and John's Gospel quotes Psalm 69:9: 'Zeal for your house will consume me' (REB).

What Hosea wanted, and what God wanted (and always wants), is to bless and to satisfy. A lover always wants to be the source of the beloved's satisfaction and happiness, and the delight is mutual. We hardly dare to believe that we can be a source of delight to God, but it says that we are. When God created the world, Wisdom was there with him 'delighting in the sons of men' (Proverbs 8:31, RSV). And the New Testament tells us that Christ is the wisdom of God, and that it was through Christ that God made the world.

Reflect

What would you like God to do for you—and for your nation? What would it be like to be really satisfied—not with food and drink but with God? We are created for union and communion with God—and it is only the love of God that can ever totally satisfy our hearts.

Joel 2:23–27 (GNB)

Renewed and restored

'Be glad, people of Zion, rejoice at what the Lord your God has done for you. He has given you the right amount of autumn rain; he has poured down the winter rain for you and the spring rain as before. The threshing places will be full of corn; the pits beside the presses will overflow with wine and olive oil. I will give you back what you lost in the years when swarms of locusts ate your crops. It was I who sent this army against you. Now you will have plenty to eat, and be satisfied. You will praise the Lord your God, who has done wonderful things for you. My people will never be despised again. Then, Israel, you will know that I am among you, and that I, the Lord, am your God and there is no other.'

Last summer I moved to Oxford during a heatwave and a drought. Port Meadow, the local common land, is nearby, and the whole meadow was brown and parched. The river was low, and the cows and horses that graze there had no pasture. But now, after a week's rain, the grass is green again and the animals are feeding again. The grass grows up from the roots, right at the bottom of the plant—and spiritual growth always springs from the roots. For the people of Zion the renewed rain was the outward sign of an inner renewal of their fellowship with God, and the things that they had lost were being restored to them.

For some of us the years in our past seemed to be wasted years. We were separated and cut off from the love of God. Or we felt as if we were. The reality was that the love was always there, pursuing us and wooing us, but we had either separated ourselves from the relationship or else never entered into it. Yet in the providence of God those years are not wasted. He uses them in the making and remaking of us. When I first read 'I will give you back the years which the locust has eaten' (RSV) I believed that they were the words of God to me, and a promise of what he would do in the future. And he has done for me just what the words say. Other people I know have believed them in the same way and had the same experience. In the providence of God nothing is wasted—and whatever happened in our past can be used to enrich our present.

Reflect

Our spirits are dry because they forget to feed on you.

St John of the Cross

Joel 2:28–32 (GNB)

Anointed and Christed

'Afterwards I will pour out my spirit on everyone: your sons and daughters will proclaim my message; your old men will have dreams, and your young people will see visions. At that time I will pour out my spirit even on servants, both men and women. I will give warnings of that day in the sky and on the earth; there will be bloodshed, fire, and clouds of smoke. The sun will be darkened, and the moon will turn red as blood before the great and terrible day of the Lord comes. But all who ask the Lord for help will be saved. As the Lord has said, "Some in Jerusalem will escape; those whom I choose will survive." '

Jesus was the Christ, the anointed one, and he was anointed for a purpose, and he said what it was: 'The Spirit of the Lord is upon me, because he has anointed me to preach good news to the poor. He has sent me to proclaim release to the captives and recovering of sight to the blind, to set at liberty those who are oppressed...' (Luke 4:18, RSV).

But one day other people as well as the unique Son of God would be anointed with the Spirit of God. This prophecy of Joel was quoted by Peter on the Day of Pentecost—and the promise was made to every person in every generation: 'to you and your children, and all who are far away' proclaimed Peter (Acts 2:39, GNB). And that means us in our generation just as much as those first Christian believers in theirs. We are anointed— and we are 'Christed'—men and women alike, to proclaim the message and the good news of the love of God.

We don't all have to be preachers, but we do all have to be able and ready to say what the message is. 'Be ready at all times to answer anyone who asks you to explain the hope you have in you', says Peter (1 Peter 3:15, GNB). And Paul tells the believers to 'do everything without complaining or arguing, so that you may be innocent and pure as God's perfect children, who live in a world of corrupt and sinful people. You must shine among them like stars lighting up the sky, as you offer them the message of life' (Philippians 2:14–16, GNB).

But God loves the world of corrupt and sinful people, and Christ died for them.

To think about

You are anointed and Christed. Pray for a fresh anointing so that you can offer the message of life to a sad and needy world.

Joel 3:12–15 (GNB)

Judgment, love & freedom

'The nations must get ready and come to the Valley of Judgement. There I, the Lord, will sit to judge all the surrounding nations. They are very wicked; cut them down like corn at harvest time; crush them as grapes are crushed in a full winepress until the wine runs over.'
Thousands and thousands are in the Valley of Judgement. It is there that the day of the Lord will soon come. The sun and the moon grow dark, and the stars no longer shine.

'Your will be done,' Jesus told us to pray—and if the will of God was always done then Jesus would have been wasting his words to say what he did and we would be wasting our time to pray as he told us.

'It is not his will that any should be lost, but that all should come to repentance,' it says in 2 Peter 3:9 (REB)— but before that the writer says that some will be lost, because not all will come to repentance. 'By God's will the present heavens and earth are being reserved for burning; they are being kept until the day of judgement when the godless will be destroyed.'

The will of God is that the godless should repent, and be godly, and be forgiven, and be loved. The will of God is that they should be redeemed, and live with him for ever in the glory of heaven. But the will of God is not always done—since he has created the human race with free will: to accept his love and forgiveness and to say 'Yes' to God, or to reject his love, refuse forgiveness, and say 'No' to God. Even God cannot *make* people love him.

We don't like the idea of judgment, or the thought that some people in the world will be lost and cast into what Jesus described as 'the outer darkness'. But not liking something, or not believing something, doesn't mean that it won't happen. We can be wrong—and we can't say that we haven't been warned.

To think about

Think about the day of the Lord and the day of judgment. Think about the One who will be our judge. Think about Jesus weeping over Jerusalem. Think about the will of God. Think about the love of God.

Joel 3:16–21 (GNB)

Alternative endings

The Lord roars from Mount Zion; his voice thunders from Jerusalem; earth and sky tremble. But he will defend his people. 'Then, Israel, you will know that I am the Lord your God . . . At that time the mountains will be covered with vineyards, and cattle will be found on every hill; there will be plenty of water for all the streams of Judah. A stream will flow from the Temple of the Lord, and it will water the Valley of Acacia. Egypt will become a desert, and Edom a ruined waste, because they attacked the land of Judah and killed its innocent people. I will avenge those who were killed; I will not spare the guilty. But Judah and Jerusalem will be inhabited for ever, and I, the Lord, will live on Mount Zion.'

Our destiny is to enjoy God's presence for ever—and he will enjoy our presence. The lush vineyards and the flowing streams are a symbol of full satisfaction: 'when I awake, I shall be satisfied with seeing your likeness' (Psalm 17:15, NIV)—and on the final day, and for all eternity, the sons and daughters of God will be like Christ: 'we know that when he appears, we shall be like him, for we shall see him as he is' (1 John 3:2, NIV).

Then sin will be banished for ever, and so will the causes of sin. Joel's readers would have recognized Egypt as a regular cause of their own spiritual defeat, and Edom as their greatest enemy. So Egypt and Edom are symbols too, and these causes of trouble to the people of God will finally be destroyed. But there are two possible endings to every human life. One is to be with Christ for ever. The alternative ending is destruction. St Paul writes about both endings—and what he says is our final reflection.

Consider

God will do what is right: he will bring suffering on those who make you suffer, and he will give relief to you who suffer and to us as well. He will do this when the Lord Jesus appears from heaven with his mighty angels, with a flaming fire, to punish those who reject God and do not obey the Good News about our Lord Jesus. They will suffer the punishment of eternal destruction, separated from the presence of the Lord and from his glorious might, when he comes on that Day to receive glory from all his people and honour from all who believe. You too will be among them, because you have believed the message that we told you.

2 Thessalonians 1:6–10 (GNB)

John 16:21–24 (NIV)

Death and birth

'A woman giving birth to a child has pain because her time has come; but when her baby is born she forgets the anguish because of her joy that a child is born into the world. So with you: Now is your time of grief, but I will see you again and you will rejoice, and no-one will take away your joy. In that day you will no longer ask me anything. I tell you the truth, my Father will give you whatever you ask in my name. Until now you have not asked for anything in my name. Ask and you will receive, and your joy will be complete.'

The Bible often uses the imagery of childbirth to signify the birth into eternity. Here it is linked to Jesus' death in an ironic and paradoxical way. Jesus is speaking to his disciples on the night before he died about being born. The night of the last supper when he was so cruelly betrayed by a disciple is the moment he chooses to tell them of his loyalty. He will see them again.

In the holy communion service I find similar paradoxes. There's fellowship. We congregate and share news. We have come for a meal like the disciples did and it's good to be together. Yet the centre-piece of the table is a symbol of execution, a cross. There's tremendous awe as we realize that the God who created the vast universe is present. Yet the youngest of children can approach him more easily than I can. There's profound sadness as we discover that even today we need forgiveness for our wrongdoing. That meant the pain of the cross for our Saviour. And yet there's immense joy as we see the risen Jesus amongst his people.

All these emotions are evident in our worship and can sometimes be somewhat bewildering. In some ways that is how mothers-to-be feel. It's also how the disciples felt too. What's happening? What's going to happen next? Where am I?

And throughout Jesus says, 'I will see you again.' His reassuring tones come just at the point when we need them most and suddenly we know we are in good hands. His words ring out of the reading in the service. His love pours out, overwhelming our lives. He never stops giving as he tells his disciples over and over again to ask and receive. As my hands accept the symbols of his love, I ask, I receive and my joy is complete.

GD

John 14:15–17 (NRSV)

Obedience brings blessings

[Jesus said:] 'If you love me, you will keep my commandments. And I will ask the Father, and he will give you another Advocate, to be with you forever. This is the Spirit of truth, whom the world cannot receive, because it neither sees him nor knows him. You know him, because he abides with you, and he will be in you.'

The next two weeks' readings are on the theme of the Holy Spirit and are taken from the Gospel of John, with two related readings from the First Letter of John. We begin today with the conditions for receiving the Holy Spirit: love and obedience.

Obedience isn't a popular word in modern thinking. But it determines our relationship with God. Jesus himself came to 'do the will of the Father', and it was as he perfectly fulfilled the Father's will that the blessings of God flowed through him into the life of the world.

We too are called to lives of obedience—not the blind, unthinking obedience of fear, but the willing, glad obedience of love. Just as the lover is desperate to do what the beloved wants ('Tell me to jump off a cliff and I will!'), so the true disciple shows love for God by doing his will.

So the words of Jesus are not so much an instruction as a description: If you love me, you will keep my commandments. The one is the consequence of the other.

But there is a further consequence of this willing obedience. Jesus will 'ask the Father', and in response to that request the Father will give us 'another Advocate', the 'Spirit of truth'.

An advocate is someone who is on our side, who represents and supports us. The imagery is of the law court, and I imagine it's an enormous relief if you are in the dock that among all the bewigged figures who look so daunting there is one in the court who is 'on your side'—your advocate.

The Holy Spirit is our 'advocate'. He stands by us, our permanent helper and enabler. He is on our side, even when circumstances, people and the world itself seem to be against us.

And the 'price' of this gift? Obedience!

A reflection
Help me gladly to obey your will, and gratefully to accept your gift— the Holy Spirit, the promised Helper.

John 14:18–21 (NRSV)

Not left as orphans

[Jesus said:] 'I will not leave you orphaned; I am coming to you. In a little while the world will no longer see me, but you will see me; because I live, you also will live. On that day you will know that I am in my Father, and you in me, and I in you. They who have my commandments and keep them are those who love me; and those who love me will be loved by my Father, and I will love them and reveal myself to them.'

Being 'orphaned' must be an appalling experience. The word comes from Greek, where it means 'desolate, bereft'—and that's just what a child is who is suddenly without the parents upon whom it has depended. Jesus realized that that was how his disciples would feel when he had gone. They had depended on him, relied on him, drawn on his strength. How could they cope if he were suddenly taken away from them? This passage is his answer.

He would not leave them 'orphaned'. He would come to them. He would not come as he had done over the past couple of years, sitting with them at breakfast, walking along the lanes of Galilee with them—or even appearing miraculously alongside them when a storm threatened to sink their boat. But he was leaving them in order to be present with them in a different but more powerful way. That's the mystery of the ascension and of Pentecost.

In these verses he explains how the mystery would come about. He was returning to the Father, and they would recognize his special relationship with the Father. But because they loved him, and he was loved by the Father, they would then be in a new relationship of love with God.

In this relationship, Jesus would not just be alongside them, like a companion, but within them, like an indwelling presence: 'I in my Father, you in me, and I in you.' Far from being deprived of the presence of Jesus, the promise was that he would be with them—and us—in a new and better way.

A reflection

When I feel 'orphaned'—when I lose my awareness of your loving care and strength for me—help me to experience through the Spirit the reality of his life within me.

John 14:25–26 (NRSV)

The divine reminder

[Jesus said:] 'I have said these things to you while I am still with you. But the Advocate, the Holy Spirit, whom the Father will send in my name, will teach you everything, and remind you of all that I have said to you.'

It's common ground to all Christians that the Bible is 'inspired', but people have argued about what that means in practice. Where the Gospels are concerned, for instance, does it mean that through divine inspiration we can have access to the exact words that Jesus spoke so long ago, precisely as he said them? And if it doesn't, in what way are the Gospels 'inspired'?

Jesus points out that for a couple of years the disciples have had the benefit of his teaching. Now he is going. But God's gift, the 'Advocate', the Holy Spirit, would be an even more effective teacher than he had been. The reason? Because the Holy Spirit would operate within them, he could teach them 'everything'—rather like having a personal tutor and coach at hand day and night.

Not only that. They might forget what Jesus had taught them—that would only be human. But the Holy Spirit would 'remind' them of everything he had said. So the Holy Spirit is the clue to the inspiration of the New Testament writers, because Christ's followers would be guided by the Spirit to recollect reliably all that he had taught them.

Now we know from our own reading of the Gospels that that doesn't mean that they give us his exact and precise words. If that were so, one Gospel would have been enough. The writers weren't word processors! But the Holy Spirit would ensure that what they recorded was 'true'—that it expressed the truth about Jesus. So this is a remarkable promise, which became the basis of the Church's acceptance of the Gospels as part of the inspired scriptures. It should also shape our attitude to them: reverent, receptive, obedient.

A reflection

May the Holy Spirit, who guided the human writers of the Gospels, also guide us as we read them, so that their words may be to us the word of God.

John 14:27–29 (NRSV)

The Spirit of peace

[Jesus said:] 'Peace I leave with you; my peace I give to you. I do not give to you as the world gives. Do not let your hearts be troubled, and do not let them be afraid. You heard me say to you, "I am going away, and I am coming to you". If you loved me, you would rejoice that I am going to the Father, because the Father is greater than I. And now I have told you this before it occurs, so that when it does occur, you may believe.'

The Holy Spirit is not only the Spirit of unity, as we've seen, and the guarantor of truth, but the source of real peace. 'Peace'—*shalom* in Hebrew—was (and still is) the normal greeting in Israel. But what Jesus offered his followers was more than the mere formality of a customary greeting ('not as the world gives...'). He gave them not just 'peace', but his peace, a peace which the circumstances of life or the ups and downs of their feelings couldn't affect.

This peace was also the Father's peace—and 'the Father is greater than I'. Jesus as a man operated within the confines of human life and experience; the Father who sent him ruled the universe. What greater guarantee of peace could they ask than that based on the authority of the Creator of everything that exists?

It was also the Spirit's peace, because it would be confirmed to them as they saw what he had foretold coming true—and his words, as we have seen, would be 'brought back' to them by the Spirit.

That's still true for us, of course. As we see the over-arching purpose of God at work in our lives—in the details as well as in the broad pattern—we recognize that he does what he says. We may not always see it at the time—the disciples didn't—but when we do, it is a great source of inner peace. We are not victims of a meaningless chance, but children of a Father who knows our path before we tread it.

A reflection

Spirit of peace, give me the peace that comes from knowing that the future, as well as the past, is in the hands of a loving heavenly Father.

Acts 1:1–11 (NRSV)

Ascension Day

In the first book, Theophilus, I wrote about all that Jesus did and taught from the beginning until the day when he was taken up to heaven, after givng instructions through the Holy Spirit to the apostles whom he had chosen. After his suffering he presented himself alive to them by many convincing proofs, appearing to them during forty days and speaking about the kingdom of God. While staying with them, he ordered them not to leave Jerusalem, but to wait there for the promise of the Father. 'This,' he said, 'is what you have heard from me; for John baptized with water, but you will be baptized with the Holy Spirit not many days from now.' So when they had come together, they asked him, 'Lord, is this the time when you will restore the kingdom to Israel?' He replied, 'It is not for you to know the times or periods that the Father has set by his own authority. But you will receive power when the Holy Spirit has come upon you; and you will be my witnesses in Jerusalem, in all Judea and Samaria, and to the ends of the earth.' When he had said this, as they were watching, he was lifted up and a cloud took him out of their sight. While he was going and they were gazing up towards heaven, suddenly two men in white robes stood by them. They said, 'Men of Galilee, why do you stand looking up towards heaven? This Jesus, who has been taken up from you into heaven, will come in the same way as you saw him go into heaven.'

Today is Ascension Day, so we have an extra reading to celebrate the day and to meditate on the meaning. So spend some time thinking about the passage.

Jesus had convinced the apostles and the disciples that he was alive. He had spoken to them after his death and resurrection. Now he was going away—in one form—but he would come to them in another. The Holy Spirit—his Spirit, and the Spirit of God—would come to them and dwell in them.

Now they were to wait for that to happen. Then they would have power, and be witnesses to Jesus. He had gone 'into heaven'—but he would still be with them. And he is with us. And we are with him—and in him—in heaven.

Think about that—and pray to understand more of the mystery.

SB

John 15:26–27 (NRSV)

Counsel for my defence

[Jesus said:] 'When the Advocate comes, whom I will send to you from the Father, the Spirit of truth who comes from the Father, he will testify on my behalf. You also are to testify because you have been with me from the beginning.'

Today we think of the Holy Spirit as the 'Advocate', which is how most modern versions translate the Greek word *parakletos*. The King James Version, of course, has 'Comforter', which was fine when the word had its original meaning ('one who gives us strength'), rather than the implication of soothing and making comfortable which the word has today.

An advocate—a barrister who represents us in court, for instance—is someone who acts in our defence, who's on our side and pleads our cause. But *parakletos* conveys slightly more than that, because the root of the word is the idea of a helper, someone who renders us a service.

And that is the Holy Spirit's work, in a nutshell! He has been given to stand by us, to support and strengthen us, to plead our cause and help us to live as Christians in a sometimes hostile and generally unbelieving world.

But the Spirit doesn't only speak for us, he also speaks to us. Jesus said, 'He will testify on my behalf'—to Christians, and to the world. The Holy Spirit is the great evangelist, the only true

preacher, the source of all honest witness. And whenever we are called to evangelize, preach or witness, we shall only be able to do so effectively if he is within us.

So when Christians are called to 'testify', as we are from time to time, that testimony is really the work of the one Spirit—the Spirit who 'testifies' on behalf of Christ (v. 26). Recognizing that may help us to be less nervous about it!

A reflection

Lord Jesus, thank you for the Father's gift of the advocate, who speaks on my behalf and offers me help, support and guidance. May I draw on his strength, lean on his support and follow his words of guidance, for your name's sake.
Amen.

John 16:5–7 (NRSV)

Gaining by losing

[Jesus said:] 'But now I am going to him who sent me; yet none of you asks me, "Where are you going?" But because I have said these things to you, sorrow has filled your hearts. Nevertheless I tell you the truth: it is to your advantage that I go away, for if I do not go away, the Advocate will not come to you; but if I go, I will send him to you.'

In his brief ministry—probably less than three years—Jesus was able to visit several parts of Palestine, talk to many thousands of people, heal hundreds, and make a handful of disciples. In one sense, it's not a lot to show for the impact of the most remarkable life ever lived.

So it is understandable that he wanted his disciples to realize that this was just the beginning. His ministry would culminate in the events of Holy Week. The salvation of humankind would be achieved—Jesus would have 'completed the work which the Father had given him to do' (see John 17:4).

But the work of drawing the whole world into that salvation remained—and humanly speaking it was going to be left to this rather pathetic band of disciples. His leaving was to their 'advantage', he said, because only when Jesus had returned to the Father would the Holy Spirit be given to them. And it was by the Spirit, and only by the Spirit, that they could possibly tackle the task that they were being given.

And so it proved. By the power of the Holy Spirit the infant Church carried the gospel to every part of the Roman Empire, and far beyond. They reached infinitely more people, and won infinitely more disciples, than the human Jesus did. As he said, they would do 'greater works' . . . because he had returned to the Father.

And it's still true. The Holy Spirit continues to reach people with the gospel and to make disciples in every nation. And it is still to our advantage that Jesus returned to the Father, and gave us this most precious of all gifts.

A reflection

Thank you, O my Father,
for giving us your Son,
And leaving your Spirit
till the work on earth is done.

Melody Green
© Cherry Lane Music 1982

Ephesians 4:1–6 (NRSV)

We are one in the Spirit

I therefore, the prisoner in the Lord, beg you to lead a life worthy of the calling to which you have been called, with all humility and gentleness, with patience, bearing with one another in love, making every effort to maintain the unity of the Spirit in the bond of peace. There is one body and one Spirit, just as you were called to the one hope of your calling, one Lord, one faith, one baptism, one God and Father of all, who is above all and through all and in all.

We've been reading from St John, in these days leading up to Pentecost, but today it's St Paul—part of the Epistle for the Sunday after the Ascension.

He invites us to think about the Holy Spirit in terms of his effect. Jesus compared the Spirit to the wind—you can't see the wind, but you can see what it does. The Holy Spirit isn't a theory, but a person who does things.

And first and foremost he is, as the creed says, 'the giver of life'. 'There is one body and one Spirit', says Paul—the capital 'S' may disguise the meaning of the picture. A body is merely a cadaver without breath, and the Greek word for 'Spirit' (with or without a capital!) is *pneuma*, which simply means 'breath'. The Holy Spirit is the breath of God bringing life to what was dead—to dead hearts, dead relationships, dead congregations. Without the Holy Spirit religion is just struggle and a 'church' is just an empty shrine. It is the 'breath of God', the Holy Spirit, who gives life—and renews life, when it seems to be fading!

He also unites us. The Holy Spirit is the Spirit of unity, because all who share the life of God have that life in common, whatever labels or denominations they go under. But this is not only true of churches. True Christian unity is more fundamental than that. It is a deep, God-given unity in all our relationships, based on 'humility, gentleness, patience, forbearance' (v. 2)—and a genuine effort to forge with 'bonds of peace' the unity that the Spirit gives (v. 3).

A reflection

May the Holy Spirit who gives us life also give us love, so that we may enjoy unity with God and with one another. Amen.

John 16:12–14 (NRSV)

A guide for the journey

[Jesus said:] 'I still have many things to say to you, but you cannot bear them now. When the Spirit of truth comes, he will guide you into all the truth; for he will not speak on his own, but will speak whatever he hears, and he will declare to you the things that are to come. He will glorify me, because he will take what is mine and declare it to you.'

This passage (and you can helpfully include the next verse, v. 15, if you like!) tells us what it is that the Spirit has been given to declare. The Holy Spirit is the 'Revealer' of the Godhead—it's his task to make things known, to explain and reveal what God wants his people to know. That's why he's spoken of as the source of the scriptures (2 Timothy 3:16; 2 Peter 1:21). But he is also their interpreter. Without the help of the Holy Spirit, the truths of God would be a closed book to us.

So the 'Spirit of truth' will guide us into 'all the truth'. That implies that the disciples didn't have it yet! For them there lay ahead a painful and long process of learning—learning what the cross and resurrection were to mean, for instance. And the Spirit was to be their teacher.

He was also to be their guide, and that promise is as much to us as to them. There can't be many people who haven't from time to time felt a desperate need for a guide through the darker paths of life. That guide is the 'Spirit of truth'. He takes us by the hand and leads us through the maze of difficulty, and because he is the Spirit of truth he is an utterly reliable guide.

He also guides the Church. God has not finished that process of teaching us, nor have we completed the process of learning! In each generation the people of God need the guiding hand of the Spirit of truth. Woe betide a Church that thinks it has nothing left to learn!

A reflection

The Spirit of truth lead you into all truth, give you grace to confess that Jesus Christ is Lord, and to proclaim the word and works of God.

Alternative Service Book

John 16:20–22 (NRSV)

A secure joy

[Jesus said:] 'Very truly, I tell you, you will weep and mourn, but the world will rejoice; you will have pain, but your pain will turn into joy. When a woman is in labour, she has pain, because her hour has come. But when her child is born, she no longer remembers the anguish because of the joy of having brought a human being into the world. So you have pain now; but I will see you again, and your hearts will rejoice, and no one will take your joy from you.'

These marvellous words were in answer to the disciples' bafflement at the idea that they would 'no longer see' Jesus, and yet, after a little while, they would see him (see vv. 16–19). It was true that he would be taken from their sight, and that that would be a very painful experience—as indeed it was. What he wanted them to know was that that pain would be turned to a very special kind of joy when eventually he would see them again.

Jesus' description of the pain, and then the joy, of childbirth will mean more to mothers than to the rest of us! But we can all see the power of the illustration. Life begins in pain, but within a few moments it is turned to joy. I'm told that the pain of childbirth is actually quite extreme, but tends to be forgotten in the unequalled joy of the birth of a child. It will be like that for the disciples. The pain of the cross will be turned very quickly into the joy of the resurrection and the continuing presence of Jesus through the Holy Spirit.

What Jesus says of childbirth and labour is true of so much human experience. A cosy, protected life may be largely free from pain, but it is unlikely to know true joy, either. The old hymn speaks of the 'joy that seekest me through pain'. It is a profound truth. And that kind of joy no one can take from us.

A reflection

Help me, Lord, to discover that deep joy which shines through the dark experiences of life—the joy that is the empty tomb after Calvary.

John 16:23–24 (NRSV)

The true way to ask

[Jesus said:] 'On that day you will ask nothing of me. Very truly, I tell you, if you ask anything of the Father in my name, he will give it to you. Until now you have not asked for anything in my name. Ask and you will receive, so that your joy may be complete.'

This is one of those sayings which is simple enough on the surface, but full of deep implications. Why will they 'ask nothing' of Jesus 'on that day'— that is, the day of joy, when they will meet Jesus again ... the day of resurrection and the gift of the Spirit? The answer is in the verb 'to ask', which here carries the meaning of 'enquire'. On 'that day' all their questions and doubts will be answered.

On the other hand, they will ask— not questions, but requests. And from now on they will ask in the most effective way open to human beings: 'in my name'. Up to now, their prayers had been those of devout Jews, bringing their requests to God in the hope that, according to his will, he would grant them. But 'on that day', in the new world brought about by the coming of the Holy Spirit, they would be able to pray 'in the name of Jesus', guided and directed by his Spirit. And that prayer will always be granted by the Father.

All of us are familiar with the idea of ending our prayers with the phrase 'through Jesus Christ our Lord' or 'in the name of the Lord Jesus'. But to pray 'in the name of Jesus' implies much more than the addition of a few words! It means that we are praying, or seeking to pray, within his will and according to his purpose. To ask 'in the name of Jesus' is to ask as his 'representative' (which is what the phrase means)—to ask what he would ask if he were where we are. To act in someone's 'name' is to act with their authority, and prayer 'in the name of Jesus' has his authority.

No wonder, therefore, that it is answered. And no wonder that it brings complete joy.

A reflection

True prayer originates in the will of God, is expressed by the lips of human beings, is heard at the throne of grace and is effective in the creation. The right way to ask is to ask for what is right.

John 16:32–33 (NRSV)

The secret of security

[Jesus said:] 'The hour is coming, indeed it has come, when you will be scattered, each one to his home, and you will leave me alone. Yet I am not alone, because the Father is with me. I have said this to you, so that in me you may have peace. In the world you face persecution. But take courage; I have conquered the world!'

Here, on the eve of the awful events that will terrify and scatter the disciples, Jesus let them into the secret of true security. It did not lie in circumstances, because 'in the world you face persecution'. Indeed, at least ten of those listening to him were to die for the faith over the succeeding years, and they would all suffer at the hands of God's enemies. And it did not lie in some extraordinary quality of courage of their own: 'you will leave me alone'—'the disciples all forsook the Lord and fled'.

Instead, it lay entirely in the security of the Trinity. Jesus would not be 'alone' because the Father would be with him. And with the Father and the Son would be the irresistible power of the Holy Spirit, carrying out the divine purpose in the world. The strength of God is the unity of the Trinity.

So their peace was not to be found in circumstances, but 'in me': 'in me you may have peace'. That peace which Jesus knew as a member of the Trinity could also be theirs. Just as the Father was in him, and he in the Father, so they were to be in him, and he was to be in them. This is the recurrent message of chapters 13–17 of John's Gospel. Christ's followers are 'in' him, united to him. They live in him and, through the Holy Spirit, he lives in them.

And that is the source of peace. The world around may roar and threaten, but to those who are 'in Christ' it can do no lasting harm. The roars are the roars of a dying beast. The threats are the threats of a disarmed foe. Take courage: 'I have conquered the world!'

A reflection

Turn my eyes, heavenly Father, from all the things around that terrify me, and fix them on your strength.

1 John 4:13–16 (NRSV)

Abiding in love

By this we know that we abide in him and he in us, because he has given us of his Spirit. And we have seen and do testify that the Father has sent his Son as the Saviour of the world. God abides in those who confess that Jesus is the Son of God, and they abide in God. So we have known and believe the love that God has for us. God is love, and those who abide in love abide in God, and God abides in them.

As we turn from John's Gospel to his First Letter, we find the same theme: the unity of the believer with the Holy Trinity. We dwell in Christ and he dwells in us, which means that we are united to God himself. We have been 'given' the Spirit, it says, and 'God abides in those who confess Jesus'. It is a truly staggering notion—people no better than we are being united with the Creator of the universe.

But there is a new element here. 'God is love.' That is not quite the same as saying 'God loves' or 'God is loving'. It is the remarkable claim that the One who is the origin of everything that exists, the source of life itself and the very purpose of the creation, is love. It is his nature. He is love in the way that water is hydrogen and oxygen, or stone is hard.

So all that we have read of the coming of God to us, as his Son for salvation, and as his Spirit as our advocate and helper, is in essence the coming of pure Love. That is presumably why those who have a profound encounter with God invariably de-scribe it as an overwhelming sensation of being loved, and of expressing love. If God is love, that is no more than we should expect.

God's love is not sentimental or self-indulgent, as human 'love' often is. It is demonstrated, John says, by the gift of his Son. In other words, it is a self-giving love and a sacrificial love. Those who abide in God (which is all those who confess Jesus as Lord) share in that love, receiving it, and, of course, expressing it. What a calling!

A reflection

God loves, God is loving, God is love. Meditate on the meaning of each of those three statements. And think of his two great gifts of love, his Son and his Spirit.

1 John 5:6–8 (NRSV)

The true witness

This is the one who came by water and blood, Jesus Christ, not with the water only but with the water and the blood. And the Spirit is the one that testifies, for the Spirit is the truth. There are three that testify: the Spirit and the water and the blood, and these three agree.

One New Testament scholar has called this 'one of the most perplexing passages in the New Testament', so don't be surprised if you found it a bit baffling! Yet it is important, because it emphasizes that it is the Holy Spirit who is the true witness to Jesus Christ. Men and women are his witnesses, of course, but the only utterly reliable witness to Jesus—who he is, and what his coming meant—is the Holy Spirit, 'the truth'.

And the truth to which he testifies is that Jesus 'came by water and blood'—a strange phrase! In the account of the crucifixion in John's Gospel the writer makes quite a point of the 'water and blood' that came from Jesus when his side was pierced (John 19:34–35). Obviously this phenomenon had a deep and mysterious significance. The words 'water' and 'blood' conveyed some essential truth about the meaning of the gospel.

The 'water' probably refers to baptism—the baptism of Jesus which marked the start of his ministry. In that baptism, he identified himself with the whole of mankind in their need of God's forgiveness and new life. Yet at the same moment the Spirit testified that 'this is my beloved Son'.

The 'blood' undoubtedly refers to the cross, which marked the end of his earthly ministry, where by the death of the Son of God forgiveness and new life were made possible. So 'water' and 'blood' are a kind of shorthand for the whole purpose of Christ's coming to earth, confirmed by the witness of the Holy Spirit through the Church. Thus the writer answered the heresy of the Gnostics, which this letter was written to refute. Jesus was truly man and truly God—from Jordan to Calvary, inclusively!

A reflection

'Water' and 'blood' can also speak to us of the two Gospel sacraments, baptism and the eucharist. But only the Holy Spirit can make even those sacraments true witnesses to Jesus. Without him, they are empty symbols.

John 20:21–23 (NRSV)

Pentecost

Jesus said to them again, 'Peace be with you. As the Father has sent me, so I send you.' When he had said this, he breathed on them and said to them, 'Receive the Holy Spirit. If you forgive the sins of any, they are forgiven them; if you retain the sins of any, they are retained.'

Some people have called this 'John's Pentecost'—his description of how the Holy Spirit came to the disciples. It happened in the evening of the day of the resurrection, what we now call Easter Day. The risen Jesus appeared among his disciples in the locked upper room and identified himself by the marks of the crucifixion which he still bore. Convinced that it was Jesus, the disciples 'rejoiced'.

Then Jesus commissioned them to the task that lay ahead. In the same way as the Father had sent him, so he was sending them. He had been sent 'to the lost sheep of the house of Israel'. They were to be sent to the whole world. He had been sent to 'serve, and to give his life as a ransom for many'. They also were to go out in loving and sacrificial service, to declare to the whole of mankind the glorious news of what that 'ransom' had achieved.

But they needed a new strength to do it—they needed the promised 'advocate' or 'helper', of whom we have been reading over the past fortnight. So he 'breathed' on them, the breath of the Spirit of God: 'Receive the Holy Spirit . . .'

He told them that their mission was a mission of judgment and salvation. Through their message some would find forgiveness and—sadly—some would reject it. His call here is not to ordination to some special priestly caste (though if it were, it certainly included women—see v. 18!), but to the mission which is shared by the whole Church, and is for the whole world.

Here the Holy Spirit comes as a gentle breath, the breath of Jesus. At Pentecost he came as roaring wind and blazing fire. Both are ways in which the Spirit may come to us. For some, the 'still, small voice'; for others, the erupting power: but for all, the same promised gift of the Father.

A reflection

This Pentecost, may I be open to the Spirit of God, however he comes to me—quietly and secretly, or powerfully and publicly. Come, Holy Spirit!

DW

Genesis 22:9–10 (NIV)

Abraham and Isaac

Abraham built an altar there and arranged the wood on it. He bound his son Isaac and laid him on the altar, on top of the wood. Then he reached out his hand and took the knife to slay his son.

When our first child was born, I remember gazing through the glass wall of the 'baby ward' at this little scrunched-up person. I'd never experienced the kind of love I felt at that moment. It was different from anything I felt for family, friends or even my wife—not more, just different. It filled me with a determination to care endlessly for his welfare, a determination that, as most parents know, doesn't lessen with the years.

At the same time, I had been spiritually 'raised' in a climate of self-sacrifice and denial. God had to come first, and the setting aside of strong feelings for friends or family was regarded as a positive virtue. The story of Abraham being asked to sacrifice Isaac just made me feel sick. A shadow fell over my perception of the relationship I had with God, because I knew that I would never sacrifice Matthew, neither actually nor symbolically. How could I, when I loved him much more than I loved the Creator of the world? Inwardly, I flirted with atheism, preferring the prospect of human relationships followed by oblivion, to the shift in priorities that God seemed to be demanding.

The journey from that state of mind to my present one is too long and eventful to describe here, but some things I now know to be true. First, God stood beside me outside that baby ward, excited like me about the arrival of someone who was as much a new son for him as for me. His commitment to caring for Matthew was and is endless too, in the literal sense. Secondly, my love for my son has changed. It's more about him and less about me. I *want* him to enjoy eternal life. I *want* him to walk through the streets of heaven with a brand-new, indestructible body. I want him to be a child of God above anything else. Thirdly, perhaps most importantly, I have come to understand a little better what I would, with great respect, call the 'sanity' of God. He knows me and my weaknesses and strengths, and has done since the day when he chuckled fondly outside the baby ward where *I* was born. He has been a good and very wise Father, and, as that fact becomes real to me, I come closer to loving him more than anyone in the world.

Prayer

Father, I'm a long way from trusting you as Abraham did. Help me to learn that trust is the best way for me, and thank you for sacrificing your own Son so that mine can live.

2 Samuel 12:19–20 (NIV)

David

David . . . realised that the child was dead. 'Is the child dead?' he asked. 'Yes,' they replied, 'he is dead.' Then David got up from the ground. After he had washed, put on lotions and changed his clothes, he went into the house of the Lord and worshipped. Then . . . he ate.

David's response to the death of the child conceived in his adulterous relationship with Bathsheba says something very profound about his understanding of God. He prayed and wept for seven days and nights, but when the child died, he accepted the judgment of the Lord. David loved God. His relationship was a *real* one. In crunch situations the reality of what we believe makes a demonstrable difference—or not, of course. A friend of mine, who was a traffic warden, recently died in hospital of cancer, amazing visitors with a new strength and authority as he approached his death. He really wanted to be healed, but he was ready to accept the will of the God he trusted. For his funeral service I wrote and read the following lines:

He stood at the crossroad of his own life
Directing the traffic of emotions, thoughts, events
Too watchful once, perhaps
For woe betide some maverick urge that tried to jump the queue
And overtake good common sense that ought to set the pace
He tried, he really tried to set his face against irregularity
Longed to see the day when all of life's unruly streams
Would be reorganised into an earthly paradise of dead straight lines
With no untidy tailbacks to upset him
Alas for all his dreams, his bosses wouldn't let him
He had three bosses
One in heaven, one in Hastings, one at home
The first and last of these instructed him in many things
They taught him that the waving through of tender thoughts
A blind eye turned when unashamed compassion
Does a sudden U-turn in the outside lane
Need not be crimes
That facts and feelings have to double-park sometimes
And in the end, in the main, love was flowing freely
Far too soon, far too soon for us, the traffic noises died
And on that soundless day
A chauffeur-driven certainty came softly in the morning
And carried him away.

Prayer

Father, may we develop the kind of trust in you that upheld these two men who worshipped the same God. We want it to be real, Lord.

Genesis 7:11–12 (NIV)

Noah

In the six hundredth year of Noah's life, on the seventeenth day of the second month—on that day all the springs of the great deep burst forth, and the floodgates of the heavens were opened.

A friend, whom I shall call Herbert, told me once about an encounter over coffee with someone whom I shall call Bertha. For some reason my name or one of my children's names came up in the conversation.

'Do you know the Plasses?' asked Bertha, settling into an I've-got-something-to-say sort of posture.

Herbert, who isn't a Christian but knows us very well, was quite unable to resist the temptation to find out what Bertha was going to say, and replied vaguely, 'Well—you know, I've come across them. Why do you ask?'

'You want to be very careful there,' replied Bertha darkly. 'Don't get more involved than you absolutely have to.'

Herbert was deeply intrigued to hear us talked about as though we were some sort of suspect political movement. 'Why do you say that?' he enquired innocently. 'Is there something wrong with them?'

'They're religious fanatics!' announced Bertha dramatically. 'They want to draw other people in, that's all they're interested in.'

'I didn't realize you knew them,' said Herbert.

'Oh, I've never spoken to them,' said Bertha, 'but it's common knowledge.'

Bertha wasn't very sure of her facts, but I found it interesting that 'common knowledge' held us to be fanatics—weirdos whose lives were centred on something not of this world. I would hate those who really know us to describe us in that way, but I guess it's inevitable that those who have heard and believed in the approach of a great disaster, and the possibility of great salvation, will seem slightly strange to the rest of the world. That's why nominal religion is such a crime. True Christianity might appear bizarre in some ways, but at least people notice it and wonder why it's there.

Few of us will be called upon to look quite as ridiculous as Noah must have appeared, but let's value our divine foolishness a little more than we have in the past. When the great rain of judgment comes, we won't look weird any more, and we might even have been able to hand out a few spiritual umbrellas in advance.

Prayer

Father, it's so hard to get the balance right between openness about what we believe, and normal contact with the world. Give us courage and good judgment.

Job 29:21–24 (NIV)

Job

'Men listened to me expectantly, waiting in silence for my counsel. After I had spoken, they spoke no more; my words fell gently on their ears. They waited for me as for showers and drank in my words as the spring rain. When I smiled at them, they scarcely believed it; the light of my face was precious to them.'

Job is one of my heroes, not just because his regard for God survived poverty, skin disease and extremely annoying friends, but because of the kind of man he was. The content of this passage, a description by Job himself of the way in which his counsel was received by others in pre-boil days, is the target at which I unsuccessfully aim in my writing and speaking. This servant of God clearly brought three things straight from the heart of God to all those who listened.

(I can't believe I'm about to make three points about something. Perhaps I should get out of the Anglican Church before it gets even worse.)

First, he says that his words fell 'gently' on their ears. Oh, for a few more gentle words in church. Many of the people I encounter have already been bruised by bawled accusation and crushed by echoing admonition. Jesus could be very tough, but he felt such compassion for the crowds. He still does, so let us all be gentle on his behalf, unless we're very specifically called to behave in some other way.

The second thing is about the showers and the spring rain. Job helped his listeners to feel refreshed and lightened in spirit. They would have felt *more* able to cope after hearing him, not less. Forgive me for repeating one of my constant bleats, but the blessing of God does not discourage and disable me, it makes me feel that I might be able to get somewhere after all.

The last bit is my favourite. When Job smiled at them they could hardly believe it. I cannot adequately express the sheer delight I have experienced on those few (too few) occasions when I have seen some frightened face suddenly illuminated by the awareness that God is actually *smiling* at his nervous, guilt-racked son or daughter. They can hardly believe it! God is nice! Why did no one ever tell them?

Prayer
Father, help our gentle words to bring the refreshment of your smile to those of your children who need it.

Genesis 3:16–19 (NIV)

Adam and Eve

To the woman he said, 'I will greatly increase your pains in childbearing; with pain you will give birth to children. Your desire will be for your husband, and he will rule over you.' To Adam he said, 'Because you listened to your wife and ate from the tree ... cursed is the ground because of you; and through painful toil you will eat of it all the days of your life ... By the sweat of your brow you will eat your food until you return to the ground, since from it you were taken; for dust you are and to dust you will return.'

I'm not sure if it's legitimate to feel sorry for Adam and Eve, but I always have done. Imagine facing up to the fact that you and your spouse are entirely responsible for every single problem faced by each and every one of countless billions of people throughout the history of the world. Can't you just picture this fig-leaved couple waiting red-faced and awkward just inside the gates of heaven to greet each newcomer with an apology and, perhaps, and apple?

'Sorry,' they would say, as the line of saints winds slowly past them, 'we honestly and truly are *very* sorry. Yes, ha, ha, you've got it—Adam and Eve, that's right. Yes, yes, we did make a bit of a mess of it—well, not a *bit* of a mess, more of a total mess. Still, it all worked out okay in the end, didn't it? Well, it did for you, anyway. No thanks to us, that's right—sorry again, see you later. Good morning to you! I'm Adam, and this is my wife Eve—I beg your pardon? Err, no, no, not mythical guilt symbols at all. We wish! Much rather we hadn't existed ourselves, to be absolutely honest. Both world wars and every ingrowing toe-nail there ever was—down to us, I'm afraid. Deeply sorry. Have an apple? No, well, can't say I blame you... Good morning to you! This is Eve and I'm Adam—responsible for the Fall, that's right—spot on. Well, both of us really—you don't like to apportion blame, do you? You had what? A difficult time with your third one? We genuinely are most terribly sorry ...'

Whether or not we subscribe to the view that there really was a real Adam and a real Eve, who transgressed with a real apple after being tempted by a real serpent, we would do well to focus on our own real contribution to the fallenness of this world. There is only one official scapegoat, and I am quite sure that he definitely existed. Let us acknowledge the apple-sampling rogue that lies within each of us, and thank God for Jesus, the new Adam.

Prayer

Thank you for Jesus, who fixed it for us.

2 Samuel 11:11 (NIV)

Uriah the Hittite

Uriah said to David, 'The ark and Israel and Judah are staying in tents, and my master Joab and my lord's men are camped in the open fields. How could I go to my house to eat and drink and lie with my wife? As surely as you live, I will not do such a thing!'

There are some memories that we fight to avoid, aren't there? In my own case, they are mainly recollections of those occasions when one of my children has been suddenly hurt or deeply upset about something, and especially when that hurt involved a significant erosion of their naturally optimistic view of the world. I hate it. When those memories surface, particularly late at night, my heart sinks and I pray that some bright distraction will soon lighten my darkness.

Other memories, however, are to do with my own misdoings. Even though God long ago forgave me for certain sins, I still experience a sickness in my spirit when I am forced for some reason to look at those dark things.

I am quite sure that the memory of Uriah's enthusiasm and loyalty haunted David for the rest of his life. He murdered that good man to cover up his own adultery. That's the trouble with sin committed by big-hearted people. Such folk throw themselves into wrongdoing with the same abandonment that is evident in their acts of generosity and goodness. Layer after layer of deceit is laid down until only an explosion of evil or an act of incredibly brave disclosure

will change the situation. David managed (goodness knows how, when he knew God so well) to kid himself that he would get away with sin of the worst kind, simply because he had managed to hide his crimes from men. In the end, he had to face God, of course, through the prophet Nathan, and although he was forgiven, the consequences of his sin were appalling. I really do find it extremely difficult to read about David's agony of spirit over his son Absolom.

Please, if you are involved in wrongdoing that is bound to end up hurting people who are close to you, or the God who loves you more than you can imagine, *do* something about it now. Take the brave option rather than the evil one. Easy to say, I know, but we'll pray with you now.

Prayer

Father, some of the people who are reading this note today are getting themselves into a lot of trouble. A world of remorse lies ahead. Please give them the courage to battle their way out of the darkness and into the light. It will be very tough, but you will be with them, and so, in spirit, will we. Thank you, Father.

John 14:13–17 (NIV)

Trinity Sunday

'I will do whatever you ask in my name, so that the Son may bring glory to the Father. You may ask me for anything in my name, and I will do it. If you love me, you will obey what I command. And I will ask the Father and he will give you another Counsellor to be with you for ever—the Spirit of truth.'

Being brought up as a Catholic in a Catholic school I was drilled in religion every day. One of the themes was the oneness of God and the threeness of God. 'This', the Mother Superior told us constantly, 'is a mystery and shall always remain a mystery.'

There was something about the mystery which was intriguing. My friends and I in junior school could not fathom it and yet neither could we leave it alone. We kept talking about it and, just as we thought we'd got it all sorted out, it eluded us again. I think this was the first time I had fun with God in a mental way. It was like a spiritual game of tag, as his truth ran round the corner just as I was about to catch it.

I thought I'd lost that type of thinking until recently when someone asked me to pray for them. He wanted guidance for his future. We prayed together, and I became aware of God giving me a picture, but it was right at the corner of my eye. It was so far to the side I couldn't make it out. God was doing it again. The mystery was not going to be solved without a chase, so we prayed on. I kept trying to follow this image until eventually it came into view quite clearly. As it was private I will not say what it was. But the point was that God and I had played a mystery game.

God is mysterious and works in mysterious ways. A member of my congregation found that out when he drove home from work one night and said, 'Dear God it would be great if it were mushrooms for tea tonight.' He then turned the corner where a lorry had shed its entire load of mushrooms! He thankfully collected them up and laughed as he thought of the verse in our reading, 'You may ask me for anything and I will do it.'

Trinity Sunday celebrates a deep mystery. Let's enjoy it.

GD

Malachi 1:1–4 (REB)

Love and anger

An oracle. The word of the Lord to Israel through Malachi. I have shown you love, says the Lord. But you ask, 'How have you shown love to us?' Is not Esau Jacob's brother? the Lord answers. Jacob I love, but Esau I hate, and I have reduced his hill-country to a waste, and his ancestral land to desert pastures. When Edom says, 'We are beaten down, but let us rebuild our ruined homes,' these are the words of the Lord of Hosts: If they rebuild, I shall pull down. They will be called a country of wickedness, a people with whom the Lord is angry for ever.

The book of Malachi was written nearly 2,500 years ago, but its message is timeless, and just as relevant to us in our generation as it was to them in theirs. It is a message about judgment and repentance, so that the people who hear the message and obey it can be blessed.

'God and Malachi wanted a righteous nation; a pure and devoted priesthood, happy homes, God-fearing children, and a people characterized by truth, integrity, generosity, gratitude, fidelity, love and hope' (Robert L. Alden in *The Expositor's Bible Commentary*, page 704).

'Malachi' means 'messenger', and one of the ways he communicates his prophetic message is by asking questions and then answering them. Sometimes it is the Lord who asks the question, sometimes the people. The starting point of the prophecy is the beautiful declaration from God that 'I have shown you love.' But the people dispute that. Things haven't been going well for them, and they think that if God really loved them then things would be much better than they are. Malachi will be telling them in the rest of his prophecy just why things are going badly, but the Lord's answer to 'How have you shown love to us?' is to tell them how he will conquer their long-time enemy, Edom.

'Jacob I love, but Esau I hate' is a Hebrew idiom for saying that Jacob is chosen, or preferred, rather than Esau. Hard on Esau, maybe, but Jacob passionately wanted to be chosen, whereas Esau sold his birthright for a meal of delicious-smelling stew. In this note it isn't possible to discuss the statement that the Edomites are a people 'with whom the Lord is angry for ever', but the cause of the anger has to be that they are 'a country of wickedness'.

Reflect
Read the quotation from Robert Alden again and reflect on it.

Malachi 1:6–14 (REB)

It's you that he wants . . .

A son honours his father and a slave his master. If I am a father, where is the honour due to me? If I am a master, where is the fear due to me? So says the Lord of Hosts to you, priests who despise my name. You ask, 'How have we despised your name?' By offering defiled food on my altar. You ask, 'How have we defiled you?' By saying that the table of the Lord may be despised . . . Better by far you should close the great door altogether, to keep fire from being lit on my altar to no purpose! I have no pleasure in you, says the Lord of Hosts, nor will I accept any offering from you . . . You profane me by thinking that the table of the Lord may be defiled, and you can offer on it food that you hold in no esteem. You sniff scornfully at it, says the Lord of Hosts, and exclaim, 'How tiresome!' If you bring as your offering victims that are mutilated, lame, or sickly, am I to accept them from you? says the Lord. A curse on the cheat who pays his vows by sacrificing a damaged victim to the Lord, though he has a sound ram in his flock! I am a great king, says the Lord of Hosts, and my name is held in awe among the nations.

If anyone should have known the Law it was the priests. They were the last people on earth who should have permitted blind, lame or sickly animals to be offered as sacrifices. It was forbidden in Deuteronomy 15:21, and to permit it was to despise the holy name of God. Because of this God says that they might as well close their temple services down and shut up shop.

The questions at the start of today's passage should have brought the people up short, if they really considered them. 'Where is the honour due to me?' 'Where is the fear due to me?' And the answer was 'Nowhere.' The Lord of Hosts wasn't being honoured, or feared. He was being despised, and their attitude was totally unacceptable.

To think about

What do you offer to God of your life—your time, your love, your money? Spend some time thinking about it, and about what Paul wrote to the Christians in Rome: 'Therefore, my friends, I implore you by God's mercy to offer your very selves to him: a living sacrifice, dedicated and fit for his acceptance, the worship offered by mind and heart' (Romans 12:1).

Malachi 2:1–8 (REB)

Good and bad priests

And now, you priests, this decree is for you: unless you listen to me and pay heed to the honouring of my name, says the Lord of Hosts . . . I shall turn your blessings into a curse . . . and I shall banish you from my presence. Then you will know that I have issued this degree against you: my covenant with Levi falls, says the Lord of Hosts. My covenant was with him: I bestowed life and welfare on him, and laid on him the duty of reverence; he revered me and lived in awe of my name. The instruction he gave was true, and no word of injustice fell from his lips; he walked in harmony with me and in uprightness, and he turned many back from sin. For men hang on the words of the priest and seek knowledge and instruction from him, because he is the messenger of the Lord of Hosts. But you have turned aside from that course; you have caused many to stumble with your instruction; you have set at naught the covenant with the Levites, says the Lord of Hosts.

The priests were supposed to instruct the people in the faith, and they were supposed to be the guardians of religious truth and learning. But instead of building people up in the faith they were pulling them down. They were not like Levi, the founding father of the levitical priesthood and one of the twelve sons of Jacob whose new name was Israel. Joel describes the way that Levi lived, and the consequence of his living: that 'he turned many back from sin'.

That is what those priests were meant to do—and it is what all Christians are meant to do. Through the old covenant the Lord of Hosts 'bestowed life and welfare' on Levi, and through the new covenant he has done the same for us, in an even better way.

'The days are coming,' says the Lord, 'when I shall establish a new covenant with the people of Israel and Judah . . . I shall set my law within them, writing it on their hearts; I shall be their God, and they will be my people. No longer need they teach one another, neighbour or brother, to know the Lord, all of them, high and low alike, will know me,' says the Lord, 'for I shall forgive their wrongdoing, and their sin I shall call to mind no more' (Jeremiah 31:31–34).

Consider

Read about the new covenant again, and consider how true it is in your own experience. If it isn't, then pray that it might be.

Malachi 2:10–12 (REB)

Faith and faithlessness

Have we not all one father? Did not one God create us? Why then are we faithless to one another by violating the covenant of our fore-fathers? Judah is faithless, and abominable things are done in Israel and in Jerusalem; in marrying the daughter of a foreign god, Judah has violated the sacred place loved by the Lord. May the Lord banish from the dwellings of Jacob any who do this, whether nomads or settlers, even though they bring offerings to the Lord of Hosts.

Malachi doesn't specify what the abominable things are that are being done in Israel and Jerusalem, and we can't be sure what he meant when he said that Judah had married the daughter of a foreign god.

It could have been that Jewish men were marrying pagan wives. That was serious enough, because the pure Jewish faith would then have been corrupted by idolatry and false worship. But it could have been even more serious, in that the people of God were worshipping in pagan temples and taking part in the temple prostitution which was an essential and evil part of the worship of Baal and of Ashtoreth.

Paul picks up the same idea in 2 Corinthians 6:14–16:

'Do not team up with unbelievers. What partnership can righteousness have with wickedness? Can light associate with darkness? Can Christ agree with Belial, or a believer join with an unbeliever? Can there be a compact between the temple of God and idols? And the temple of the living God is what we are.'

These can sound harsh directions in our tolerant, twentieth-century world, and most of us have known extreme and rigid Christians who have been fierce and exclusive and anything but Christlike and loving.

The mother of a friend of mine refused ever to eat with her and her husband because they had abandoned that particular brand of Christianity and joined the Church of England.

But the fact that some people have gone right over the top and have been horribly condemning to all other versions of Christianity than their own shouldn't mean that we don't pay any attention to the dangers of getting tied up with unbelievers.

To think about

If we follow Christ we shall be a friend of publicans and sinners. But we shan't marry one of them until he or she is a forgiven sinner, like us.

Malachi 2:13–16 (REB)

What divorce does . . .

Here is another thing you do: you weep and moan, drowning the Lord's altar with tears, but he still refuses to look at the offering or receive favourably a gift from you. You ask why. It is because the Lord has borne witness against you on behalf of the wife of your youth. You have broken faith with her, though she is your partner, your wife by solemn covenant. Did not the one God make her, both flesh and spirit? And what does the one God require but godly children? Keep watch on your spirit, and let none of you be unfaithful to the wife of your youth. If a man divorces or puts away his wife, says the Lord God of Israel, he overwhelms her with cruelty.

The people are weeping bitterly because God is refusing to accept their (blemished) offerings—and they are still asking why (which means they haven't been listening to what Malachi has been telling them). But there are other reasons for God's displeasure than blind and sickly sacrifices. The men are divorcing their wives—and the way Malachi writes could mean that they are getting rid of the women who have reached middle age and marrying younger women.

When Jesus said that if a man divorced his wife he caused her to commit adultery, the state of marriage in Jewish, Greek and Roman society was abysmal. Divorces were frequent and common—and a Jew could divorce his wife if she over-salted his supper, spoke rudely about her in-laws in his presence, and for several other flimsy reasons. So much so that Jewish girls were refusing to marry. In Greece and Rome it was even worse, and prostitution was part of daily life.

It was (and is) into the desolation and unhappiness that divorce so often brings about that God speaks of monogamous marriage and of faithfulness. The NIV translates the last but one sentence of today's passage as 'I hate divorce . . .', and he hates it because of the hurt that the separation almost invariably causes.

Things were far worse in those days than they are in ours, but even in England today statistics show that one in two marriages will end in divorce. God can forgive anything—and to have messed up one marriage doesn't mean that a second one cannot be greatly blessed. But from the beginning God's plan was the lifelong union of one man and one woman.

To think about

What do you think about divorce? Why do you think God speaks of it as he does?

Malachi 2:17—3:3 (REB)

Refining fire

You have wearied the Lord with your talk. You ask, 'How have we wearied him?' By saying that all evildoers are good in the eyes of the Lord, that he is pleased with them, or by asking, 'Where is the God of justice?' I am about to send my messenger to clear a path before me. Suddenly the Lord whom you seek will come to his temple; the messenger of the covenant in whom you delight is here, here already, says the Lord of Hosts. Who can endure the day of his coming? Who can stand firm when he appears? He is like a refiner's fire, like a fuller's soap; he will take his seat, testing and purifying; he will purify the Levites and refine them like gold and silver, and so they will be fit to bring offerings to the Lord.

'Where is the God of justice?' they have asked—and Malachi says that they are about to find out, because he is about to come to his temple in judgment. But with God one day is as a thousand years and a thousand years as one day, and the people who asked the question will have died by the time this prophecy has its fulfilment.

Matthew, Mark and Luke all quote the first half of 3:1: 'I am about to send my messenger to clear a path before me,' and they all make the verse refer to John the Baptist. Mark then quotes a verse from Isaiah: 'Prepare the way of the Lord, make his path straight.' It is the Lord of Hosts who will come, say the prophets. And he does—named Jesus, because he will save his people from their sins.

It is frightening to think of being put in a refiner's fire, so that the impurities in us rise to the surface and can be removed. But it isn't an impersonal fire. It is the presence of Christ himself. John sees him in the Revelation he is given on the Isle of Patmos: ' ... his eyes flamed like fire, his feet were like burnished bronze refined in a furnace, and his voice was like the sound of a mighty torrent. In his hand he held seven stars, and from his mouth came a sharp two-edged sword; his face shone like the sun in full strength. When I saw him, I fell at his feet as though I were dead' (Revelation 1:14–17).

A reflection

See in your mind's eye a picture of the risen Christ as John describes him. Stay in his presence. Know that he loves you. Then ask him to speak to you and purify you . . .

Acts 2:37–39 (NIV)

Four steps

When the people heard this, they were cut to the heart and said to Peter and the other apostles, 'Brothers, what shall we do?' Peter replied, 'Repent and be baptised, every one of you, in the name of Jesus Christ for the forgiveness of your sins. And you will receive the gift of the Holy Spirit. The promise is for you and your children and for all who are far off—for all whom the Lord our God will call.'

Peter was an extraordinary evangelist on this Day of Pentecost. The people heard what he said and were cut to the heart. It makes us preachers long for such an outpouring too. What is so admirable about Luke's account is its theological accuracy as well as its jubilant charisma. He's recording for us the way to salvation in four steps. Conveniently we have four steps in our church from the door to the holy table and I sometimes refer to them in sermons.

The first step at the door into the porch is accepting God's word. Our porch has eight sides symbolizing the newness of God (six days creating, one day off and then a new week). They were cut to the heart with this new word and wanted to know what they needed to do. Its not an easy step to take but an essential one if we want to find faith.

The second, from the porch into the church itself, is repentance. Being prepared to admit sin and say sorry is a hard step too. It involves stepping inside our lives and perhaps seeing things that have been hidden for some time.

The third is the chancel step. In Luke's account it's baptism. The chancel, where we baptize adults and babies, has a red carpet deliberately designed to symbolize the blood of Christ shed on the cross. 'Be baptised,' Peter says, 'so that your sins may be forgiven.'

Now we come to the table and the final step. This is the point at which we receive communion, and Peter's fourth step is to receive the Holy Spirit.

Each week I come through those doors and climb those steps. It's not a one-off event, although it began like that. As I come to communion these steps are important, for I shall trip if I don't observe them. Each one needs reaffirming from time to time. Some more than others, but I thank God that he has given us all a means to find faith and keep on finding it week by week.

GD

Malachi 3:6–12 (REB)

Giving for God . . .

I, the Lord, do not change, and you have not ceased to be children of Jacob. Ever since the days of your forefathers you have been wayward and have not kept my laws. If you return to me, I shall turn back to you, says the Lord of Hosts. You ask, 'How can we return?' Can a human being defraud God? Yet you defraud me. You ask, 'How have we defrauded you?' Why, over tithes and contributions. There is a curse on you all, your entire nation, because you defraud me. Bring the whole tithe into the treasury; let there be food in my house. Put me to the proof, says the Lord of Hosts, and see if I do not open windows in the sky and pour a blessing on you as long as there is need. I shall forbid pests to destroy the produce of your soil, and your vines will not shed their fruit . . . All nations will count you happy, for yours will be a favoured land.

There is hope for the sinful people of God because of the changeless nature of God. The God who is love never stopped loving the people who lived in Malachi's day, and he never stops loving us. But what doesn't change either is God's implacable hatred of sin, because it spoils and destroys the people he loves.

We are called to be holy, and to repent, for our own sake just as much as God's. He desires to have unbroken fellowship and communion with us, but our sin gets in the way. But he can deal with that—if we confess it and turn away from it. And once we know the forgiveness of God we can set about doing the will of God. For the people of Malachi's day that meant bringing the full tithes into the temple treasury. Paul wrote to the Corinthians about Christian giving:

'You are so rich in everything—in faith, speech, knowledge, and diligence of every kind, as well as in the love you have for us—that you should surely show yourselves equally lavish in this generous service! This is not meant as an order; by telling you how keen others are I am putting your love to the test. You know the generosity of our Lord Jesus Christ: he was rich, yet for your sake he became poor, so that through his poverty you might become rich' (2 Corinthians 8:7–9, REB).

Consider
Read Paul's words again—and spend some time considering your own giving.

Malachi 3:13–18 (REB)

Talking about God

You have used hard words about me, says the Lord. Yet you ask, 'How have we spoken against you?' You have said, 'To serve God is futile. What do we gain from the Lord of Hosts by observing his rules and behaving with humble submission? We for our part count the arrogant happy; it is evildoers who prosper; they have put God to the proof and come to no harm.' Then those who feared the Lord talked together, and the Lord paid heed and listened. A record was written before him of those who feared him and had respect for his name. They will be mine, says the Lord of Hosts, my own possession against the day that I appoint, and I shall spare them as a man spares the son who serves him. Once more you will tell the good from the wicked, the servant of God from the person who does not serve him.

They hadn't got it right, a lot of the people to whom Malachi was writing. They had asked fretfully what the benefits were to them of keeping the rules, when unbelievers seemed to be doing a lot better. And the unbeliever and the arrogant may have been prospering (it was the complaint of the Psalmist in Psalm 73). But these believers *hadn't* been keeping the rules. They'd been breaking them. That's what the whole thrust of the book of Malachi is about. Despising the name of the Lord and despising the covenant. Bringing in blemished sacrifices to the temple and not bringing in the full tithes. And not keeping their marriage vows. They didn't fear the Lord, so their lives had gone wrong.

But there were those who did fear the Lord, and they did what the *Shema* (the Jewish summary of belief) had always told them to do: 'Hear, Israel: the Lord is our God, the Lord is our one God; and you must love the Lord your God with all your heart and with all your soul and with all your strength. These commandments which I give you this day are to be remembered and taken to heart; repeat them to your children, and speak of them both indoors and out of doors...' (Deuteronomy 6:4–7, REB).

So the people who feared the Lord talked—and God listened.

Consider

Do you fear God in the right way? And do you talk about the things of God with other people who also fear him?

Malachi 4:1–3 (REB)

Fire and freedom

The day comes, burning like a furnace; all the arrogant and all evildoers will be stubble, and that day when it comes will set them ablaze, leaving them neither root nor branch, says the Lord of Hosts. But for you who fear my name, the sun of righteousness will rise with healing in its wings, and you will break loose like calves released from the stall. On the day I take action, you will tread down the wicked, for they will be ashes under the soles of your feet.

'Our God is a devouring fire', it says in Hebrews 12:29, and on the Day of Pentecost tongues of fire rested on everyone who was present. They were touched by God, and the Holy Spirit entered into them. As Christians we share in the divine nature—sons and daughters of the living God. So we shall be able to stand in the burning holiness of God. A hymn that I love tells of being in that presence.

Eternal light, eternal light,
How pure the soul must be,
When placed within thy searching sight,
It shrinks not, but with calm delight,
Can live and look on Thee.

The spirits that surround thy throne
May bear the burning bliss,
But that is surely theirs alone,
Since they have never, never known
A fallen world like this.

O how shall I, whose native sphere
Is dark, whose mind is dim,
Before the Ineffable appear,
And on my naked spirit bear
The uncreated beam?

There is a way for man to rise
To that sublime abode.
An offering and a sacrifice,
A Holy Spirit's energies,
An advocate with God.

These, these prepare us for the sight,
Of Holiness above.
The sons of ignorance and night
Can dwell in the eternal light
Through the eternal love.

Thomas Binney

Malachi uses a delightful image to describe what it will be like on that day for those who fear the Lord. They will gambol like calves suddenly set free from their stalls.

Imagine
Imagine being set free—and being
what you were created to be and
always yearned to be. In the holy,
burning presence of God.

Jonah 3:10; 4:1–3 (NIV)

Jonah

God . . . had compassion and did not bring upon them the destruction he had threatened . . . But Jonah was greatly displeased and became angry . . . 'O Lord, is this not what I said when I was still at home? That is why I was so quick to flee to Tarshish. I knew that you are a gracious and compassionate God, slow to anger and abounding in love, a God who relents from sending calamity.'

Of all the characters in the Old Testament the one I would most like to meet once a week in the pub is Jonah. I just know that our conversation about God, the universe and everything would be about as seamless as is possible in this fallen world. God was as much of a reality in this awkward prophet's life as a loaf of bread. Only the truest of believers would actually see the need to run away from the object of their belief purely because they knew all too well how he was likely to behave in a given situation. As for going into a sulk like a five-year-old because the *nasty-wasty people in Nineveh didn't get deaded*—well, what greater sign of faith could there be? Jonah *knew* that God was there.

The reason I mention this is that I've recently become very aware of the different ways in which people talk about God, depending on where they happen to be, and who's listening at the time. I'm sure I'm the same. In public meetings or services most of us tend to speak of our faith in definite, formal words and tones, as if doubt is a disease that very few Christians suffer from. In private, however, there is often a quite distinctly different approach to such matters, one that, in many cases, suggests that public expressions of belief might have been more optimistic and expedient than truthful.

It can be quite a shock to settle down quietly for a drink with someone only to discover that the depth of their devotion to God is as evident in their private conversation as it was in a more formal situation. I love it when it happens, but it doesn't happen very often. Very few people are as closely engaged with the person of the Father as Jonah was, whether in a positive or a negative way.

Sadly, such awareness is not as popular as one might think. The kind of true faith that has explored the whole mountain is an enormous challenge to those who have half-decided to settle for a lifetime of pottering about on the lower slopes. But it is these people, the ones who talk about God in the same breath as they talk about the price of beans, who are needed in this generation.

Prayer

Give us more prophets like Jonah, Lord, people who know you, and will argue with you, and speak for you.

Haggai 1:3–8 (NIV)

Haggai

Then the word of the Lord came through the prophet Haggai: 'Is it a time for you yourselves to be living in your panelled houses, while this house remains a ruin? . . . Give careful thought to your ways. You have planted much, but have harvested little. You eat, but never have enough. You drink, but never have your fill. You put on clothes, but are not warm. You earn wages, only to put them in a purse with holes in it. . . . Go up into the mountains and bring down timber and build the house, so that I may take pleasure in it and be honoured.'

When I get to heaven I shall go searching round the various mansions until I find the one with Haggai's name printed over the front porch. Then I shall knock on the door, and when Haggai opens it I shall hold out my copy of the Bible and ask him to autograph his book for me. This summary of the problems faced by a society that does not put God first is absolutely masterful. However much we have or get, in the end it's worth nothing without the one who gives.

Nowadays, we work very hard at avoiding this fact, but God has an old and experienced assistant in this area of work, and the name of that assistant is Death. In case of people like myself, the process is as follows: A queue of worries, needs and concerns occupies most of our attention for most of the time. We work very hard at shortening this queue, not least because it really is possible to deal with some of the issues. Shortage of money, for instance, can be a real problem, but it is *possible* for hard work

and a little luck to solve that problem, at least to the extent that we are comfortable. Next in the queue might be our failure to find a wife or a husband or perhaps just a good friend. Relationships can be tricky, but if we go to the right places and take a real interest in others—who knows?

Two down, 85 to go. Very few of us ever work our way through to the end of the queue, because so many difficulties and challenges are desperately hard, if not impossible, to deal with, and others tend to take their place as soon as they do disappear. Sometimes, though—just sometimes—we reach a place where, by some miracle, we find ourselves staring at the very last item on the list. Death waits quietly and confidently, the problem that cannot be solved—unless we are inhabited by the living God.

Prayer
Father, help us to make a priority of building a house for you in our hearts.

Judges 11:30–32, 34–35 (NIV)

Jephthah

Jephthah made a vow to the Lord: 'If you give the Ammonites into my hands, whatever comes out of the door of my house to meet me when I return ... will be the Lord's, and I will sacrifice it as a burnt offering.' Then Jephthah went over to fight the Ammonites, and the Lord gave them into his hands ... When Jephthah returned to his home in Mizpah, who should come out to meet him but his daughter, dancing to the sound of tambourines! ... When he saw her, he tore his clothes and cried, 'Oh, My daughter! You have made me miserable and wretched, because I have made a vow to the Lord that I cannot break.'

This little-mentioned tale contrasts bizarrely with the story of Abraham and Isaac, doesn't it? What an absolutely appalling situation! The more you think about it, the worse it gets. All I find myself able to do is ask a series of very obvious questions.

First—why did Jephthah open his big mouth and make rash promises when he didn't have to? What was the matter with him? It wasn't as if God had asked him to do it. Wild vows are dangerous, to say the least.

Secondly—what did he think was going to meet him when he returned in triumph—an earwig? Or was he perhaps expecting some more dispensable member of the household to present him or her self. If he'd asked me (granted, I wasn't around at the time) I could have told him that it's always daughters who run to greet fathers when they come home from work. He just didn't think it through, did he?

Thirdly, why didn't he break his vow and take the consequences like a man? I

don't suppose he knew what those consequences were likely to be, but if he was as fond of his daughter as he appeared to be he might have decided to find out. Instead, he killed her!

Last, but not least, why didn't God say to him, 'Look, Jephthah, old chap, let's forget that silly vow you made the other day, and just celebrate your victory over the Ammonites. I don't want your daughter to be sacrificed to me as a burnt offering—what kind of God do you think I am, for goodness sake?'

There are my questions, and I know the answers are located somewhere in the region of the ongoing revelation of the nature of God (have I got that right?), but what a story!

Prayer

Father, help us to keep our mouths shut when we're over-excited, to think things through before we make a decision, and to go on searching for the truth about who and what you really are.

Acts 4:10–12 (NEB)

The cornerstone

'It was by the name of Jesus Christ of Nazareth, whom you crucified, whom God raised from the dead; it is by his name that this man stands here before you fit and well. This Jesus is the stone rejected by the builders which has become the keystone—and you are the builders. There is no salvation in anyone else at all, for there is no other name under heaven granted to men, by which we may receive salvation.'

As we go to church today many of us will be unaware of the nuances of the building. If it is an older building we shall not have been around when the architect put his ideas down on paper or the planners accepted the design or the money was granted by the subscribers or the builders wheeled their barrows with the stones used. Yet all this had to take place in order that today we can worship in the building we normally attend.

Similarly we were not there when God planned the redemption of his people from the effects of sin. Neither were we there when the prophets foretold God's big rescue plan or when Jesus paid the price on the cross. Yet just as the building is real, Jesus' love is real and that love is the cornerstone of the Church. Rejected by his people he has now become the stone without which the structure would collapse.

As we sit in church today maybe there will be a moment for us to contemplate the building and how it speaks of care and love. Those who first wanted it to come into existence, those who designed it, those who paid for it, those who built it and those who use it are all precious to God.

In many churches today there will be healing services. Like the man in the passage who was healed, people all over the world will experience God touching their lives. But Peter wants to name the person who healed this man, it was Jesus of Nazareth. Jesus, who was rejected, now rejects no one who comes to him. Jesus, the rejected stone, has in fact become the essential rock of the Church—and Peter knew all about rocks. His name had been Simon, weak reed. But Jesus had changed him. He had given him a new name, Peter, rock. Like Jesus, he was the stuff churches are built out of.

GD

Matthew 23:1-7 (NIV)

The great hypocrisy

Then Jesus said to the crowds and to his disciples: 'The teachers of the law and the Pharisees sit in Moses' seat. So you must obey everything they tell you. But do not do what they do, for they do not practise what they preach. They tie up heavy loads and put them on men's shoulders, but they themselves are not willing to lift a finger to move them. Everything they do is done for men to see: They make their phylacteries wide and the tassels on their garments long; they love the place of honour at banquets and the most important seats in the synagogues; they love to be greeted in the market-places and to have men call them "Rabbi".'

The literal meaning of hypocrisy is 'acting the part'. Unless that is what is intended, for instance in a theatre, hypocrisy is generally frowned upon in every walk of life. The newspapers are quick to point the finger at some hypocrisy in our society and, if it is in the Church, all the better.

It is all too easy for me to allow myself to enjoy the status of a leader of society. Even though much of that leadership has been eroded there are still some who regard the clergy as special. Sometimes even congregations elevate their minister to a monster, someone who is almost God. Many a clergy marriage has been wrecked and congregations divided by such ploys of Satan.

The same is true of course for anyone who holds some kind of office. There is always the danger that we revel in the position rather than carry out the responsibility.

Jesus begins his most devastating sermon on hypocrisy by exposing the Pharisaic way of doing things and it's hot stuff! He is obviously so incensed by this religious 'lording' over people that he holds nothing back. His language is hard-hitting.

Some may decry the tabloid papers for using strong language in stories about hypocrisy in the Church. My guess is that an editor in Jesus' time wouldn't change much in this chapter before printing it. If Jesus was so angry about what was happening in his day what does he think about us today?

Contemplate

Where are the greatest hypocrisies in our world? Can I do anything about them? Where are they in my life? Can I do anything about them?

Matthew 23:13–15 (NIV)

Converted to what?

'Woe to you, teachers of the law and Pharisees, you hypocrites! You shut the kingdom of heaven in men's faces. You yourselves do not enter, nor will you let those enter who are trying to. Woe to you, teachers of the law and Pharisees, you hypocrites! You travel over land and sea to win a single convert, and when he becomes one, you make him twice as much a son of hell as you are.'

Michael Green, in his marvellous book *Freed to Serve*, which I recommend to anyone considering the ordained ministry, says that a minister is like a petrol pump attendant. She or he is there to serve those who need refreshing and should be open to everyone who wishes to replenish their fuel. It's quite clear that Jesus regarded the Pharisaic attitude as the opposite of this idea. They were élitist and exclusive and, what's more, were preventing ordinary people entering the kingdom.

Congregations can act in a similar fashion. In our diocese we have a mission initiative and the trouble with missions is that they change us. New people are added to the congregation who don't know the ropes too well. We who have been in church for some time have to make allowances.

When our children were born I had to make the same allowances. Not only did I have to get on their level to communicate but I also found that the things we used to do as a couple were rendered impossible. We used to go out on summer evenings and sit in adult company in a nice pub garden. We used to take off on the spur of the moment for a break in a tucked-away quiet hotel. All these kinds of things changed when the children came along, and rightly so. But when new converts come into old churches the reverse seems to happen. The converts get told 'we don't do that', 'you're sitting in my seat', 'you're supposed to stand and sit when the rest of us do'. In other words, be like us or else.

If we are to avoid being like the Pharisees we must be ready to be the petrol pump attendant rather than the manager of the garage. When we do that we find that the church is a dynamic, living vehicle which moves on towards a better and deeper understanding of God.

Think

What can I learn from those who are new in the church I belong to?

Matthew 23:16–19 (NIV)

Blind guides

'Woe to you, blind guides! You say, "If anyone swears by the temple, it means nothing; but if anyone swears by the gold of the temple, he is bound by his oath." You blind fools! Which is greater: the gold or the temple that makes the gold sacred? You also say, "If anyone swears by the altar, it means nothing; but if anyone swears by the gift on it, he is bound by his oath." You blind men! Which is greater: the gift, or the altar that makes the gift sacred?'

I was in a meeting the other day which was meant to be discussing a particular issue. Unfortunately, in our discussion we left the subject and started to meander down another absorbing, but irrelevant, issue. Interesting as it was, we had abandoned our aim and were diverted by this bogus issue. We became totally lost until the chairman exerted his influence and dragged us back to our aims. Many meetings have these runaway diversions.

Similarly the priests and scribes of the temple had hijacked the aims of God in his meetings with his people. They, however, did so for their own ends. Jesus uses the strongest words of authority to challenge their practices.

The leaders had corrupted the temple in two ways. First, they said that not all oaths made were heard by God, ironically especially those made in his house and closest to him—by the altar. Secondly, they encouraged oaths which lined their own pockets with gold and other gifts. No wonder Jesus says 'woe' to them.

Our Sunday school image of the Pharisees makes us condemn these corrupt religious leaders. However we don't gather the full import of this passage until we realize who the blind guides were. They were the sound religious people, part of the fabric of society, people who seemed to be helping others to get to God even if they had to indicate a little extra giving was needed. Far from being the villains of the piece they were the religious establishment who were trusted and admired. I wonder who Jesus would have picked out today as having this attitude?

Guides perceive the way and have detailed knowledge of it. Blind guides cannot even see the way. The priests and scribes controlled the way to God without even knowing how to reach him themselves.

Meditate

Do I try to control the way others approach God?

Matthew 23:23–24 (NIV)

The gnat and the camel

'Woe to you, teachers of the law and Pharisees, you hypocrites! You give a tenth of your spices—mint, dill and cumin. But you have neglected the more important matters of the law—justice, mercy and faithfulness. You should have practised the latter, without neglecting the former. You blind guides! You strain out a gnat but swallow a camel.'

I sometimes use a phrase in sermons 'when the eternal video comes out'. I imagine at some point God will look at the record of our lives and judge us on what he sees. It'll be like watching an eternal video. I remember a talk given at the end of my college days by a man who compared our lives to a film. He said it was possible to analyse a film in minute detail. We could, if we wished, analyse each dot on the screen checking it for resolution and quality. Yet even if we did this meticulously with the millions of dots in each film we would have missed the most important thing about it—its meaning.

It is possible to get caught up in the minutiae of detail about God that we miss the broad brush strokes of his will. Children are starving and being murdered on the streets of South America, thousands upon thousands of refugees are horrifically slaughtered each year, the Church is losing membership by the busload each week and yet the Western Church still slumbers. Whilst in parts of the world Christians daily risk death to follow Christ, the Church argues about secondary matters.

Jesus does not say these things are unimportant, but that we should rather work for justice, mercy and faithfulness, for these are God's will for us. These are the number-one priority for us to enact, not the minutiae which is what the Pharisees were doing.

The Aramaic words for 'gnat' and 'camel' are linguistically similar. Perhaps we would translate them 'you strain out an ant yet swallow an elephant'. If we do not enact his justice, mercy and faithfulness in our lives then maybe Jesus will ridicule our behaviour too.

Prayer

*Lord please enlarge my vision of you,
help me to see the wood from the trees,
help me to recognize the urgent and
important,
let me not give too much attention to the
unnecessary,
help me to work for justice, mercy and
faithfulness. Amen.*

Matthew 23:25–28 (NIV)

Outside in

'Woe to you, teachers of the law and Pharisees, you hypocrites! You clean the outside of the cup and dish, but inside they are full of greed and self-indulgence. Blind Pharisee! First clean the inside of the cup and dish, and then the outside also will be clean. Woe to you, teachers of the law and Pharisees, you hypocrites! You are like whitewashed tombs, which look beautiful on the outside but on the inside are full of dead men's bones and everything unclean. In the same way, on the outside you appear to people as righteous but on the inside you are full of hypocrisy and wickedness.'

Anyone who is involved in leading worship will most likely have felt at some time that they are simply acting. I remember a morning when I'd argued with my wife, shouted at my children and locked the dogs up in the cellar, all before getting to church. I was thrust into leading a congregation in worship, helping them to meet with God and outwardly express their devotion to him. Secretly, I was seething inside whilst on the outside I was looking righteous. The white surplice didn't hide much of the black cassock that morning.

Being able to match the 'inside' and 'outside' is a lifetime's endeavour but the Pharisees were not even trying. The tradition of whitewashing the tombstones in order that people would avoid the area, not touch the dead and not become ritually impure was a superficial act. Jesus reminds them that it is the inside not the outside which needs cleansing.

Once we have been washed in the waters of baptism, it's tempting to put our feet up and drink in the water of sermons, services and sacraments and try to keep the rules. The trouble is that God is in the business of changing us from within. Ironically, whilst the Pharisees were washing the kitchen pots and whitewashing the tombs to give the appearance of cleanliness, the source of Godliness had moved on. To follow Jesus means to change, and that change first of all occurs within.

It is hard to recognize all the changes God effects inside us. I would even say some of them should not be known because it would spoil them. But when our outside truly reflects what God has done within then we shall be the light he wants us to be.

Meditate

O Lord, you have searched me and you know me.

Psalm 139:1 (NIV)

Matthew 23:37–39 (NIV)

The mother hen

'O Jerusalem, Jerusalem, you who kill the prophets and stone those sent to you, how often I have longed to gather your children together, as a hen gathers her chicks under her wings, but you were not willing. Look, your house is left to you desolate. For I tell you, you will not see me again until you say, "Blessed is he who comes in the name of the Lord." '

For me, the idea of a mother hen is both reassuring and off-putting. It's reassuring because hens and mothers are protective and I like to feel secure like a chick under the wing. On the other hand, hens and mothers can be over-fussy and possessive and I don't like to be wrapped in cotton wool. However, where would we be without mothers? The answer is obviously nowhere. The unwillingness of the Jews to accept God's maternal 'gathering' left them as desolate as orphans.

Mothers who are over-fussy and possessive are trying to work something out about themselves but they work it out on their children. It may be lack of love from their partner or an insecurity inside or a need to control everything or something else—but she has no right to impose her problem on her child. That's why the child often rebels.

And what about the Church? Are we fussing about gathering everyone up, constantly trying to smarten their appearance, washing their faces, ordering them about—or are we letting God shelter them with the wings of the mother hen? Increasingly I hear of mother nature, mother earth and mother Church. But it seems to me that, until we truly sort out what Mother God is about, nature, earth and Church will simply usurp the place of God as our Creator. Indeed the New Age movement has already claimed nature and the earth as its mother.

If we really want to find the protective wing of God then we need to 'come in the name of the Lord'. In other words, commit our whole lives to serving him. 'If he's not Lord of all, then he's not Lord at all' runs the saying. He will then teach us about how God looks after his sons and daughters, and being God's only Son, he should know.

Meditate

Safe in the shadow of the Lord,
Possessed by love divine,
I trust in him, I trust in him,
And meet his love with mine.

Timothy Dudley-Smith

Luke 15:8–10 (NIV)

Search, find, rejoice

'Suppose a woman has ten silver coins and loses one. Does she not light a lamp, sweep the house and search carefully until she finds it? And when she finds it, she calls her friends and neighbours together and says, "Rejoice with me; I have found my lost coin." In the same way, I tell you, there is rejoicing in the presence of the angels of God over one sinner who repents.'

We went to church. It was a normal Sunday except that the parish all met together in St Swithin's, the parish church, in a joint service. The girls were excited about going somewhere else. Rosie and Helen, armed with blanket, chose the spot to sit, on the right side halfway down. The service had its usual style, lots of activity, even standing up to put personally written prayers beside the symbols dotted around the church. That's when it happened. The blanket disappeared. It wasn't until we were getting out of the car back at home when Helen moaned in a frighteningly panicky way, 'Where is my cuddly?' My heart sank as we contemplated hours of racking our brains, searching here there and everywhere, probably in vain, for this blanket. Why are they so important to little people?

Pauline and Rosie went into the house and Helen and I set out to find the lost security reminder. We walked up and down the pews, round the front, even in the sanctuary but was it there? No sign. We rang the wardens to find out if it had been handed in but 'no' they hadn't seen it. I even prayed to God, 'Please, I know its just a small thing but reveal the whereabouts of this blanket, will you?' I'm not sure what I was really expecting, but nevertheless I spotted a small lump in the cushion on the pew. Either one of the youth group had been messing about with the fillings again or it just could be the cuddly. I ran to the spot and almost heart in mouth lifted the cushion. There it was.

I showed it to Helen. The smile said it all—'relief, joy, I knew you would find it, you're my Dad, let me have it'. Down she ran to receive it and we hugged before going home to tell everyone.

I wonder how many people come to our churches today really searching for their security?

GD

Matthew 24:4–8 (NIV)

Signs of the end

Jesus answered: 'Watch out that no-one deceives you. For many will come in my name, claiming, "I am the Christ," and will deceive many. You will hear of wars and rumours of wars, but see to it that you are not alarmed. Such things must happen, but the end is still to come. Nation will rise against nation, and kingdom against kingdom. There will be famines and earthquakes in various places. All these are the beginning of birth-pains.'

Going into labour for the first time is arguably more frightening for the husband than the wife. I remember it well at 6.00 a.m. when Pauline woke me up with the dreaded words, 'I think I need to ring the hospital.' We rushed to the hospital and Helen was born four hours later. You just cannot tell how long the pains will last.

Birth pains are not just the physical pains of contractions, although they are the most obvious. Questions like 'What's happening to me?' 'Is everything all right?' 'Will I be OK?' also make birth nerve-racking. Jesus describes the end of the world like a birth. He paints such a vivid picture that we understand that eternal life is born with pain.

It isn't really surprising that Jesus chooses to liken the end of this present age with the birth of a child. In a sense, the period of history that we live in is rather like a pregnancy awaiting the birth into eternal life. We are alive spiritually through Christ, but between conception and birth as far as heaven is concerned.

On the other hand, we could say we've already entered eternal life. After all, Jesus did speak about being 'born again'. Many would say that the Church was born on Easter Sunday after the birth pains of Jesus' death, and baptized on Pentecost Sunday when the disciples were baptized in the Spirit. This seems to fit the events.

Daniel in his book of the Old Testament outlines these end times quite remarkably. He sees both the time just before Jesus' first coming and, coincidentally, the time before his second coming. And the remarkable thing is that there are very great similarities. As we journey through this chapter of Matthew over the next few days we shall see some of the signs of the end.

Prayer
Lord, please show me what is to come at the end so that I may not be alarmed.

Matthew 24:9–14 (NIV)

Hot growing cold

'Then you will be handed over to be persecuted and put to death, and you will be hated by all nations because of me. At that time many will turn away from the faith and will betray and hate each other, and many false prophets will appear and deceive many people. Because of the increase of wickedness, the love of most will grow cold, but he who stands firm to the end will be saved. And this gospel of the kingdom will be preached in the whole world as a testimony to all nations, and then the end will come.'

I suppose many of us wonder if we shall stand the ultimate test if it came to it. Will I be able to stand firm to the end if I have to go through this experience? The answer is unknown, for at this present time I cannot predict how I shall be in the middle of persecution. In a sense, it's a rather masochistic thought. However, what I can know is how I am today.

Two of my congregation suffered a brutal blow not too long ago. Their daughter was killed in a road accident. It was devastating and so sudden. At her funeral the words of her Baptist pastor were read out. 'In the immense tragedy of this event one thing is clear for us who continue. If there is an apology, make it today, if there is a sin, confess it today, if there is a sour relationship, heal it today, for tomorrow may be too late.'

Each day we need to keep a short account with God and our neighbours so that, when the bigger tests come, we are practised. If we are able to trust God in the day-to-day things of life then we shall equally be given the faith to cope when more major situations confront us. It was the same with the heroes of the Old Testament. Abraham's sacrifice of Isaac was not until fourteen other tests leading up to that moment were successfully completed. Daniel had to show obedience to God in the diet he ate long before he was able to face the lions.

Jesus is clear. There will be many who will loose some, even all of their love for God at the end. These will be the ones who were not prepared to stand firm in the smaller tests of faith.

Meditate

God never tests us in order that we fail, but always that we might succeed.

Matthew 24:15–19 (NIV)

The abomination

'So when you see standing in the holy place "the abomination that causes desolation", spoken of through the prophet Daniel—let the reader understand—then let those who are in Judea flee to the mountains. Let no-one on the roof of his house go down to take anything out of the house. Let no-one in the field go back to get his cloak. How dreadful it will be in those days for pregnant women and nursing mothers!'

Belshazzar's Feast—a superb piece of music by William Walton, telling the story from Daniel 5—has a most dramatic part. At the climax of the work, one word is shouted by the whole choir very loudly. Belshazzar the king has profaned the holy vessels by having an orgy, using them to get drunk. The writing has appeared on the wall and Belshazzar is judged and dies. We then hear the choir shout the word 'slain'. It's an awesome and dreadful moment in the piece, as it must have been in real life.

A similar event happened in 168BC. Antiochus Epiphanes, who is now regarded as the antichrist before the first coming of Christ, similarly profaned the temple with disgusting sacrifices. This was the abomination before the first coming. Before the second coming, Daniel predicts and Jesus points to another like the first.

The Omen, a well-known horror movie, has popularized the antichrist and possibly made him somewhat unbelievable. We must be careful not to throw out this important theme in apocalyptic writing. In the Bible the antichrist will either stand instead of Christ or be completely opposed to Christ. He will also profane as much as he can of God. John remarks on how this spirit of opposition is already roaming the earth waiting until the antichrist's arrival. I'm sure we can see this in our present age as well.

When Christians see this sign we are told to flee to the mountains. Jesus seems to suggest that some will be able to avoid the worst excesses of this desolation by getting away. However we must read the signs as they come along.

All this may sound dramatic and yet the history of human beings has been dramatic. We need look back only fifty years to see a forerunner of the antichrist making his mark.

Think

If all this was to happen as quickly as Jesus predicts, how could I be ready today?

Matthew 24:23–26 (NIV)

Easy profits, false prophets

'At that time if anyone says to you, "Look, here is the Christ!" or, "There he is!" do not believe it. For false Christs and false prophets will appear and perform great signs and miracles to deceive even the elect—if that were possible. See, I have told you ahead of time. So if anyone tells you, "There he is, out in the desert," do not go out; or, "Here he is, in the inner rooms," do not believe it.'

During the last thirty years I've noticed false prophets with their prophecies growing up inside the Church. In its 'inner rooms' of worship and its 'deserts' of poverty-area work, false prophecies as well as true prophecies have been heard side by side.

The guru mentality has been strong in the Church. There was a time when great Christian leaders would write about their 'super church' which had grown from nothing. It was made clear that there were great profits to be gained by seeking to structure a church in a similar fashion. But I also remember a leader of one of these churches say these guru figures were in very great danger of burn-out, and sadly, for some of them, the pressure was too much.

The charismatic movement introduced a kind of religious permissiveness. God poured out his Holy Spirit on his people, but some stored it in jars for a rainy day. Instead of letting the Holy Spirit pour them out for others they sat back, put their feet up, sang in tongues and revelled in their reputation.

I have also seen middle-class church people move into the urban priority areas and satisfy their need of 'helping the poor'. Not really helping the poor, but helping themselves not to feel so guilty seems to cause more harm then good.

Of course this is not new, and we study the heresies of Jesus' time and the early Church whenever we read the New Testament.

A man had inscribed on his grave: 'My grandfather preached the gospel of Christ, my father preached the gospel of socialism, I preached the gospel of science'. Times have changed us and we need to constantly look out for false gospels. There is news, good news and *the* good news and it's only *the* good news that can save us.

Think

What do I have to do to recognize something that is false or someone who is false?

Matthew 24:29–31 (NIV)

A dramatic climax

'Immediately after the distress of those days "the sun will be darkened, and the moon will not give its light; the stars will fall from the sky, and the heavenly bodies will be shaken." At that time the sign of the Son of Man will appear in the sky, and all the nations of the earth will mourn. They will see the Son of Man coming on the clouds of the sky, with power and great glory. And he will send his angels with a loud trumpet call, and they will gather his elect from the four winds, from one end of the heavens to the other.'

When Jesus died on the cross we are told that there was a great darkness covering the earth. Nature reflected what was happening in the heavens. I recollect a similar occurrence about lunchtime thirty years ago. It must have been dramatic because I was so terrified I remember it like yesterday.

When the end of the world comes, what we see and what we hear will be dramatic too. The sun, moon, stars and heavenly bodies, all things that give or reflect light, will not usurp the place of the true light that will appear. Jesus' supreme place in the order of things will be seen by all. However, not only will we see this entrance but we shall hear the trumpets.

When one principal left my music college and another was due to begin, we performed the *War Requiem* by Benjamin Britten. I remember the last rehearsal we had before we moved to the Royal Festival Hall where we were due to perform. At one point in the piece the trumpet and brass section have to play alongside the choir. We were singing very loudly and the brass came in at full pelt, double fortissimo. It was true that they had visited a hostelry shortly before the rehearsal (surprise, surprise) but their sound was at one and the same time frustrating and awesome. We were awash with sound, totally overwhelmed, it was futile trying to say anything.

I have a feeling that when Jesus returns there will be such a thrill with these trumpets we shall simply fall down on the ground. Nature and the heavens will have announced the final moments have come.

Meditate

Many people have fallen on the floor—in the Bible and since those times. The significance is what happens when they are raised up.

Matthew 24:36–37, 40–42 (NIV)

I wish we'd all been ready

'No-one knows about that day or hour, not even the angels in heaven, nor the Son, but only the Father. As it was in the days of Noah, so it will be at the coming of the Son of Man . . . Two men will be in the field; one will be taken and the other left. Two women will be grinding with a hand mill; one will be taken and the other left. Therefore keep watch, because you do not know on what day your Lord will come.'

When I was in my late teens I learnt a song called 'I wish we'd all been ready'. It was written by Larry Norman, an American songwriter, who lamented the fact that not everyone would be ready for the coming of Jesus. The song used the words of this section of the Bible.

The import of this event is its suddenness. It's the fact that we shall be going about our everyday business when Jesus comes to take us that makes it a surprise. Yet, like in Noah's time, there will be warnings.

Jesus says 'keep watch'. By this he means we should know what the likely signs of his return are and watch for them. This means that we need to be fully prepared by reading and understanding the apocalyptic writing in the Bible.

Although there are many theories about the end times it is clear that there will be an antichrist figure, a false prophet, a falling away of the people of God, and a time of trouble around the time of Christ's return. Some say Christian people will be taken to eternal life before all this, others that we shall live through it. Possibly it's better to be prepared to live through it than to assume we shall avoid it. However, the outcome is certain. Christ will win through and we shall go to be with him in paradise.

This chapter and subsequent ones of Matthew's Gospel are not meant to frighten us but rather to make us ready. A good commentary on them and other similar writings in the Bible has proved to me to be well worth reading. Like the motto of the Guides, let's 'be prepared'.

Meditate

Life was filled with guns and war,
and everyone was trampled on the floor
I wish we'd all been ready
Children died and the days grew cold,
a piece of bread could buy a bag of gold
I wish we'd all been ready.

Larry Norman

Philippians 2:6–11 (NJB)

Second Adam

[Christ], being in the form of God,
did not count equality with God
something to be grasped.
But he emptied himself,
taking the form of a slave,
becoming as human beings are;
and being in every way like a human
   being
he was humbler yet,
even to accepting death, death on a
   cross.
And for this God raised him high,
and gave him the name
which is above all other names,
so that all beings
in the heavens, on earth and in the
   underworld,
should bend the knee at the name of
   Jesus,
and that every tongue should
   acknowledge
Jesus Christ as Lord
to the glory of God the Father.

Lord Jesus Christ, in this ancient Christian hymn adopted by Paul for his letter, we see you as the Second Adam, undoing the sin of Adam. Adam was created in the form and image of God, but he tried to be equal to God; you did not see equality with God as something to be grasped and exploited. Adam tried to raise himself to the divinity, but you humbled yourself. He sought for life by his own power, but you gave up your life for us. Adam was punished by being brought low, but you were rewarded by being raised up by your Father. You were raised above all creation and given the Name above all others, so that every knee should bend at your name, and every tongue acknowledge you as they acknowledge your Father himself. You were given the divine Name of 'Lord' which may be used only of God.

This was no act of self-exaltation, but redounded to the glory of your Father. With your Father you are united in that one glory, the awesome glory so much beyond human ken that even Moses could not see it and live. You became man so that we might have a glimpse of that glory, the glory of the only-begotten Son of the Father. The glory was revealed in the hour of your cross and resurrection, when the love you bear your Father was fully revealed in your perfect act of obedience, the perfect union of your will to that of the Father in your total offering. It was for this that you were raised up, to take us with you to the fulness of life. In this we rejoice each Sunday, the day of your resurrection.

HW

2 Kings 1:9–15 (NJB)

Fire from heaven

[King Ahaziah] sent a captain of fifty soldiers with his fifty men to Elijah, whom they found sitting on top of a hill; the captain went up to him and said, 'Man of God, the king says, "Come down."' Elijah answered the captain, 'If I am a man of God, may fire fall from heaven and destroy both you and your fifty men.' And fire fell from heaven and destroyed him and his fifty men. The king sent a second captain of fifty to him, again with fifty men, and he too went up and said, 'Man of God, this is the king's order, "Come down at once."' Elijah answered them, 'If I am a man of God, may fire fall from heaven and destroy both you and your fifty men.' And lightning fell from heaven and destroyed him and his fifty men. The king then sent a third captain of fifty to him, with another fifty men. The third captain of fifty came up to Elijah, fell on his knees before him and pleaded with him . . . The angel of Yahweh said to Elijah, 'Go down with him.'

This story is not easy to stomach: had Elijah no sympathy for the captains and their fifties who were only obeying orders? Worse, had the Lord no sense of justice towards them? The background is a power-play between God and a local Canaanite god. King Ahaziah had sent messengers to consult the god of a local shrine, Baal-Zebub. Elijah blocked them and sent them back. Now that the king is summoning Elijah to explain himself, God must show by defending his messenger that he is God indeed: he does not apologize or explain!

God's people of Israel were tempted again and again to compromise. The local gods of Canaan were so attractive to them, promising prosperity of crops and children in an uncertain and unpredictable world. A little attention to them would surely do no harm! So the whole message of Elijah is that there is no compromise with the rights of God. God is absolute master. From God alone comes life and prosperity.

Pray

Master and Lord, protect me from compromise. Let me always keep clearly in sight what is right and what is wrong, and know that your rule and kingdom are all in all.

2 Kings 2:1–12 (NJB)

Elijah taken up to heaven

This is what happened when Yahweh took Elijah up to heaven in the whirlwind: Elijah and Elisha set out from Gilgal, and Elijah said to Elisha, 'You stay here, for the Lord is only sending me to Bethel'. But Elisha replied, 'As Yahweh lives and as you yourself live, I will not leave you!' . . . Elijah said to Elisha, 'Make your request. What can I do for you before I am snatched away from you?' Elisha answered, 'Let me inherit a double share of your spirit.' . . . Elijah said, 'If you see me while I am being snatched away from you, it will be as you ask . . .' Now as they walked on . . . a chariot of fire appeared, and horses of fire coming between the two of them; and Elijah went up to heaven in the whirlwind. Elisha saw it and shouted, 'My father! My father! Chariot of Israel and its chargers!' Then he lost sight of him.

These early prophets had a lonely and isolated task, standing up to kings, the leaders of God's chosen people, Israel. They were more interested in wealth and alliances than in their sacred task. Elijah and Elisha were their consciences, prodding, checking, always lurking there. Their lonely task was not to predict the future, but to be the conscience of Israel and of its king, reading events with God's own eyes, standing up for truth against compromise and evasion. So Elisha is not keen to be left on his own by his mentor, and clings to him as he knows that he is about to depart. But nevertheless his last request is not for himself but for his mission, to have the strength and insight symbolized by the spirit.

The fiery chariot (whatever that means in real terms) is God's final seal of approval on Elijah's mission, a sign that he is taking Elijah to himself. It has the same meaning as the scene which must allude to this, the ascension of Christ, when Christ is finally taken to the Father as a sign of the completion of his mission. In a non-mechanical world, fire and whirlwind are most potent signs of unstoppable power—as indeed Australian bushfires and Caribbean hurricanes remind us even today.

Pray

Father, make me alert to the prophets you send to the world today and to me in particular. Help me to see things as you see them and avoid deceiving myself to avoid your challenge.

2 Kings 4:42–44 (NJB)

The multiplication of loaves

A man came from Baal-Shalishah, bringing the man of God bread from the first-fruits, twenty barley loaves and fresh grain still in the husk. 'Give it to the company to eat,' Elisha said. But his servant replied, 'How can I serve this to a hundred men?' 'Give it to the company to eat,' he insisted, 'for Yahweh says this, "They will eat and have some left over."' He served them; they ate and had some left over, as Yahweh had said.

The striking factor in this passage is the similarity of this multiplication of loaves to Jesus' feeding of the 5,000. The writer who gave us the Gospel story in its present form (especially Mark) is obviously aware of the similarity, and recounts the event with just this series of dialogue: order—protest of impossibility—repetition of order. Finally there is the same stress on leftovers. Only Jesus' miracle is far greater: Elisha feeds 100 men with twenty 'loaves' (more like pitta bread), but Jesus feeds 5,000 with five loaves.

However, Elisha himself is already standing in the tradition of Moses, who provided bread in the desert of the exodus for his people through the power of God. The incident is shaped to show that Elisha stands in the prophetic tradition and is carrying on the office of Moses, just as the Gospel incident shows that Jesus is continuing the same tradition and is (to make a crude calculation) twenty times greater than Elisha. In the same way, Elisha's control of the same awesome power as Elijah is shown by a previous incident which we had to omit: Elijah sent down fire from heaven on soldiers sent to arrest him; when boys came and taunted Elisha for his baldness, bears came out of the forest and devoured them. This was the way of showing the power of Elijah at work in Elisha; now we see the power of Moses at work in both Elisha and—later—Jesus.

To pray

Father, you care for even the material needs of your people. If I can think of nothing else to thank you for, may I remember that even the crust of bread is a precious and wonderful gift from you.

2 Kings 5:1–15 (NJB)

Naaman the Syrian

Naaman, army commander to the king of Aram . . . suffered from a virulent skin-disease . . . Naaman came with his team and chariot and drew up at the door of Elisha's house. And Elisha sent him a messenger to say, 'Go and bathe seven times in the Jordan, and your flesh will become clean once more.' But Naaman was indignant and went off, saying, 'Here I was, thinking he would be sure to come out to me, and stand there, and call on the name of Yahweh his God, and wave his hand over the spot and cure the part that was diseased. Surely, Abana and Parpar, the rivers of Damascus, are better than any water in Israel?' . . . But his servants approached him and said, 'Father, if the prophet had asked you to do something difficult, would you not have done it?' . . . So he went down and immersed himself seven times in the Jordan, as Elisha had told him to. And his flesh became clean once more like the flesh of a little child. Returning to Elisha with his whole escort, he went in and, presenting himself, said, 'Now I know there is no God anywhere on earth except in Israel'.

The story is beautifully told (and many other charming and subtle details have here been cut out for brevity). The self-important field marshall comes with his fine retinue to find that the wretched prophet in his wretched hut does not even deign to greet him personally. Then to wash in the muddy, sluggish Jordan when he could have bathed at home in the sparkling rock-streams of Damascus, whose names roll so proudly off his lips! But it is nice to see that his servants care for him enough to call him 'Father' and to persuade him—with a little flattery!

The incident of Naaman is one of the first occasions for the spread of worship of the God of Israel beyond Israel's territorial borders. Naaman even takes two mule-loads of earth back with him, so that he can stand on the soil of Israel to pray to the God of Israel. At this time God was recognized as the saviour and protector of Israel, but his relationship to other nations was as yet unclear. The Israelites simply had not had occasion to ask the question.

Pray

Lord, make me never too proud to accept your help, to see your word in simple people and unexpected quarters.

2 Kings 9:17–24 (NJB)

Jehu

The lookout posted on the tower . . . saw Jehu's troop approaching . . . [King] Jehoram gave the order, 'Have a horseman sent to meet them and ask, "Is all well?"' The horseman went to meet Jehu and said, 'The king says, "Is all well?"' 'What has it to do with you whether all is well?' Jehu replied. 'Fall in behind me.' . . . The lookout reported, 'He has reached them and is not coming back. The manner of driving is like that of Jehu . . . he drives like a madman.' . . . As soon as Jehoram saw Jehu he asked, 'Is all well, Jehu?' 'What a question,' he replied, 'when all the while the prostitutions and . . . sorceries of your mother Jezebel go on.' At this, Jehoram wheeled and fled . . . But Jehu had drawn his bow; he struck Jehoram between the shoulder-blades, the arrow went through the king's heart and he sank down in his chariot.

The prophet Elisha has sent one of his disciples to anoint Jehu king, and now we see why. Having killed King Jehoram, he goes on to have Jehoram's mother Jezebel killed, thrown from a window by her own retinue. It was Jezebel, daughter of a priest of Tyre, where Melkart was worshipped, who had introduced multiple pagan practices and superstitions into Israel, superstitions which appealed only too easily to the populace. Pagan practices, and especially fertility rites, were continuously a danger in Israel, as the many fertility figurines and phallic symbols found by archaeologists demonstrate. We hear little of these in the Bible—only brief notices about the tolerant or reforming attitudes of kings to them—but their invisible presence, despite God's care of his people, is a warning to us about our own undetected superstitions and infidelities.

And when is violent rebellion justified? In a violent age, the Bible has no qualms about it in furtherance of religious reform. In a more sophisticated world, corruption is more insidious, and reform more complicated.

Pray

Lord, show me my own infidelities, my own superstitions and escapes from remaining true to you. Grant me to pursue justice firmly and without fear of the consequences.

2 Kings 17:13–18 (NJB)

The lessons of history

Through all the prophets and the seers, Yahweh had given Israel and Judah this warning, 'Turn from your wicked ways and keep my commandments and my laws in accordance with the entire Law which I laid down for your fathers and delivered to them through my servants the prophets.' But they would not listen, they were as stubborn as their ancestors, who had no faith in Yahweh their God. They despised his laws and the covenant which he had made with their ancestors and the warnings which he had given them . . . They . . . cast themselves metal idols, two calves; they made themselves sacred poles, they worshipped the whole array of heaven, and they served Baal. They caused their sons and daughters to pass through the fire of sacrifice . . . Because of which, Yahweh became enraged with Israel and thrust them away from him. The tribe of Judah was the only one left.

The style and attitude of this passage betray the marks of the author who composed the history of Israel. During the exile in Babylon an inspired historian collected the traditions of his national heritage, traditions about people and places, oral traditions handed down for generations, and royal records inscribed in the palace archives. In the exile Israel was dominated by a crippling sense of guilt: through their unfaithfulness, God had been forced to abandon the promise he had made always to protect his people. The historian saw the history of Israel in a series of four movements: first Israel was *unfaithful* to God. Then God responded by allowing invaders to *punish* them. This led to Israel's *conversion* and return to God. So finally he *rescued* them.

The chief fault was lack of trust in the Lord, turning to other gods and superstitions for insurance. The most horrific was human sacrifice, 'causing their sons and daughters to pass through the fire of sacrifice', recorded in the Bible on a few occasions of crisis: you buy off a vengeful deity at the price of a child.

What would the lines be of a religious history of modern times? Double-dealing and heroism, cynicism and generosity, broken promises and self-sacrifice, national betrayals and individual faithfulness?

Pray

God, let me put my trust ultimately only in you, not in the passing values of your created universe. Give me the wisdom to see what is truly valuable and the courage to pursue it.

Colossians 1:15–20 (NJB)

Head of the body

[Christ] is the image of the unseen
  God,
the first-born of all creation,
for in him were created all things
in heaven and on earth . . .
all things were created through him
  and for him.
He exists before all things
and in him all things hold together,
and he is the Head of the Body,
that is, the Church.
He is the Beginning,
the first-born from the dead,
so that he should be supreme in
  every way;
because God wanted all fullness to
  be found in him
and through him to reconcile all
  things to him,
everything in heaven and everything
  on earth,
by making peace through his death
  on the cross.

Lord Jesus Christ, before time began
you were the first-born of all creation,
in whom all things came to be. You are
the Wisdom of God. By means of this
image your servants in the Old Testament sought to express God at work in
the world, but not absorbed or tainted
by it. They represented you as a
reflection of the eternal light, the
untarnished mirror of his active
power. With our limited minds we
can attempt to express your relationship to the Father only by such inadequate imagery. As God's Wisdom you
are *of* the Father, yet not *identical with*
the Father. You are our way to the
Father, our mediator.

Through your resurrection you are
also the first-born from the dead, the
first-born of the new creation and the
completion of creation, the end-point
to which it tends. You reconcile all
things to the Father. As head of the
body you provide guidance and good
sense to the Church, the body which
you nourish and cherish. In my selfish
way, my body, my self, is important to
me in a way that nothing else is; this
care you lavish on us, your body, with
affectionate attention. This gives me
dignity and importance, but also responsibility: as a member of your body
I must do your work, accept the direction and nourishment flowing from the
head. You must be the brains and
planning behind me, the principle
which makes sense of my existence
and gives everything cohesion.

In a way you are nearer to me than I
am myself. You combine the dignity of
being keystone of creation with the
individual care for each member of
your body. Help me to stay always
united to you.

HW

2 Kings 18:9–16 (NJB)

Invading Samaria & Judah

In the fourth year of Hezekiah . . . Shalmaneser king of Assyria marched on Samaria and laid siege to it. He captured it after three years . . . The king of Assyria deported the Israelites to Assyria and settled them in Halah on the Habor, a river of Gozan, and in the cities of the Medes. This happened because they had not obeyed the voice of Yahweh their God and had broken his covenant, everything that Moses servant of Yahweh had laid down . . . In the fourteenth year of King Hezekiah, Sennacherib king of Assyria advanced on all the fortified towns of Judah and captured them. Then Hezekiah king of Judah sent this message to the king of Assyria at Lachish, 'I have been at fault. Call off the attack, and I will submit to whatever you impose on me.' The king of Assyria exacted three hundred talents of silver and thirty talents of gold . . . and Hezekiah gave him all the silver in the Temple of Yahweh and in the palace treasury . . . Hezekiah stripped the facing from the leaves and jambs of the doors of the Temple . . . and gave it to the king of Assyria.

After the moral has been pointed out comes the blow. First the northern kingdom of Israel was sacked. Assyrian empire-building policy was to deport the population of lands they overran to other countries, so that they lost their local loyalties and became reliant only on the empire. So the northern tribes disappear from history, and their place in Samaria is taken by deportees from elsewhere. Their faith was not strong enough to survive this shock, and we hear no echo of continued loyalty to Yahweh in their land of exile.

The southern kingdom of Judah, though further away from Assyria than Israel, had already paid tribute as 'protection money'. But Hezekiah took the opportunity of a change of monarch in Assyria to assert his independence. Sennacherib rapidly put paid to that by sacking all the cities of Judah, leaving Jerusalem 'like a hut in a cucumber field', as Isaiah says. Now Hezekiah commits his ultimate betrayal: by buying Assyria's protection he has already shown that he places no trust in God's protection. Now he strips God's temple in order to pay his gigantic fine.

Pray

God, give me faith and trust in your protection, even when things go wrong. You never abandon us. I need only grasp the lifeline you dangle before me.

2 Kings 18:17–27 (NJB)

Sennacherib's envoy

From Lachish the king of Assyria sent the cupbearer-in-chief with a large force to King Hezekiah in Jerusalem . . . He summoned the king. The master of the palace . . . the secretary and the herald . . . went out to him. The cupbearer-in-chief said to them, 'Say to Hezekiah, "The great king . . . says this: What makes you so confident? Do you think empty words are as good as strategy and military strength? . . . You may say to me: We rely on Yahweh . . . But have his high places . . . not been suppressed by Hezekiah? . . . I will give you two thousand horses if you can find horsemen to ride them." ' . . . [They] said to the cupbearer-in-chief, 'Please speak to your servants in Aramaic, for we understand it; do not speak to us in the Judean language within earshot of the people on the ramparts.' But the cupbearer-in-chief said . . . 'On the contrary, [my lord sent me here] to the people sitting on the ramparts who, like you, are doomed to eat their own dung and drink their own urine.'

This story seems to have occurred during the Assyrian invasion of yesterday's reading; this is the only Assyrian invasion of Judea mentioned in their careful royal military records. It must form part of the negotiations. The Judeans vainly try to persuade the envoy to speak in the diplomatic language of the Near East, Aramaic, which the Hebrew-speaking common people will not understand. He sensibly but inconveniently insists that his lurid threats of the horrors of siege need to be heard by the common people, precisely to lower their morale. He wants to make clear that there is no hope for Jerusalem.

In fact Assyria withdrew from besieging Jerusalem at the last minute. The Bible says the angel of the Lord struck down 185,000 Assyrian soldiers. Greek sources hint at a similar extraordinary event: rats ate their bowstrings. Whatever the facts, this withdrawal was regarded as evidence of the miraculous protection of God. Certainly, the mildness of a fine as a punishment for Hezekiah's rebellion is unprecedented in Assyrian records. The eye of faith is justified in seeing the protecting hand of God.

Pray

God, open my eyes to see your protecting hand lurking behind the events of daily life. Help me to remember that there is no such thing as blind chance, but that you protect continuously those who try to put their trust in you.

2 Kings 20:12–18 (NJB)

The lure of Babylon

At that time the king of Babylon, Merodach-Baladan . . . sent letters and a gift to Hezekiah, for he had heard of his illness and his recovery. Hezekiah was delighted at this, and showed the ambassadors his entire treasury, the silver, gold, spices, precious oil, his armoury too, and everything to be seen in his storehouses . . . The prophet Isaiah then came to King Hezekiah and asked him, 'What have these men . . . seen in your palace?' 'They have seen everything in my palace,' Hezekiah answered. 'There is nothing in my storehouses that I have not shown them.' Then Isaiah said to Hezekiah, 'Listen to the word of Yahweh. "The days are coming when everything in your palace, everything that your ancestors have amassed until now, will be carried off to Babylon. Not a thing will be left . . . Sons fathered by you will be abducted to be eunuchs in the palace of the king of Babylon."'

This is the first contact with the rising power of Babylon. Its king was trying to lure Assyria's vassals and allies away from their allegiance as part of his campaign to achieve independence. In barely a century Babylon would have taken over the position of Assyria as the greatest power in the Near East, and would—as Isaiah warns—have first subdued and then sacked the city of Jerusalem, and the people gone into captivity in Babylon.

Hezekiah's trouble was that he was too pleased with himself. He trusted in his own power and wealth, showing them off to the ambassadors, instead of relying only on the protection of God. The exact date of this incident is uncertain, and the Babylonian movement to shake free of Assyria may have been the occasion of Hezekiah's own move, which provoked such quick reprisal. But Hezekiah also had good qualities; he was a religious reformer and abolished idolatrous cults. When he was gravely ill he turned to the Lord, and was cured against all hope. This ability to trust the Lord is seen as the reason why the destruction of Jerusalem was postponed for another century, for the course of history was seen as directly moved by the hand of God, rewarding virtue and punishing evil.

Pray

Not to us, Lord, not to us,
but to your name give the glory,
for your faithful love and your
constancy.

2 Kings 23:1–24 (NJB)

The reforms of Josiah

[King Josiah] then had all the elders of Judah and of Jerusalem summoned to him, and the king went up to the Temple of Yahweh with all the people of Judah and all the inhabitants of Jerusalem . . . In their hearing he read out the entire contents of the Book of the Covenant discovered in the Temple . . . The king ordered Hilkiah with the priest next in rank and the guardians of the threshold to remove all the cult objects which had been made for Baal, Asherah and the whole array of heaven; he burnt them outside Jerusalem in the fields of the Kidron and had the ashes taken to Bethel. He exterminated the spurious priests whom the kings of Judah had appointed . . . And from the Temple.. he took the sacred pole outside Jerusalem . . . and . . . he burnt it . . . He pulled down the house of the sacred male prostitutes which was in the Temple . . . The king gave this order to the whole people, 'Celebrate a Passover to Yahweh your God, as prescribed in the Book of the Covenant.' No Passover like this had ever been celebrated since the days when the judges ruled Israel.

Some seventy years after Hezekiah's reforms, King Josiah again cut back the luxuriant growth of idolatry in Israel. He abolished the fertility cults of the 'high places' on the mountain-tops, and stripped the sacred objects which had crept even into the temple (and would do so again after his reforms). Baal and Asherah are ancient Canaanite gods, of thunder and fertility respectively; the 'sacred pole', ancestor of our maypole, was also a male fertility symbol. It is striking to see how easily the true worship of God became contaminated with other cults and superstitions which the people found attractive.

The inspiration for this reform came from the book of Deuteronomy, discovered in the course of repairs to the temple at this time. Perhaps it had been planted there. In the version we now have (it was re-edited later) it is the perfect combination of law and love, insisting that God's Law is the revelation of his love, and that obedience to the Law is no drudgery, but is the willing response of love.

Pray

You must love Yahweh your God with all your heart, with all your soul, with all your strength.

Deuteronomy 6:5

2 Kings 24:10–16 (NJB)

First deportation into exile

At that time the troops of Nebuchadnezzar king of Babylon advanced on Jerusalem, and the city was besieged. Nebuchadnezzar . . . advanced on the city and his generals laid siege to it. Johoiachin king of Judah—he, his mother, his retinue, his nobles and his officials—then surrendered to the king of Babylon, and the king of Babylon took them prisoner . . . [He] carried off all the treasures of the Temple . . . and the treasures of the palace and broke up all the golden furnishings which Solomon king of Israel had made for the sanctuary . . . as Yahweh had foretold. He carried all Jerusalem off into exile, all the nobles and all the notables, ten thousand of these were exiled, with all the blacksmiths and metalworkers; only the poorest people in the country were left behind . . . All the men of distinction, seven thousand of them . . . all the men capable of bearing arms, were led off into exile in Babylon by the king of Babylon.

Exile is still a phenomenon today, with all its horrors of loss of house, job, possessions, hope and future. The horror of this exile is hard to overestimate, for everything in which Israel trusted was lost. Not only had they lost everything and been dragged hundreds of miles across the arid desert to a foreign land, foreign worship, foreign gods, foreign culture. Worse still, their life had been centred on the temple and its worship. By his covenant in the desert of the exodus, God had promised to protect his people always, and for centuries he had prospered them. The symbol of that protection was his presence in the temple and the guidance of his representative, the king.

They had, of course, been warned, as the biblical author quietly hints by his 'as the Lord had foretold'. Too late

they could see the inevitable consequences of their idolatry, infidelity and reliance on other props such as foreign alliances. It was not because their God was too weak to protect them. Rather they had persistently broken his covenant till he could disregard this no longer. The guilt added to their bewilderment and misery as they journeyed into exile.

This first exile was intended only to prevent any chance of revolt again. A puppet state still remained, a puppet king without weapons, without arms-manufacturers, without soldiers.

Reflect

By the rivers of Babylon we sat and wept at the memory of Zion.

Psalm 137:1

SATURDAY 13 JULY

2 Kings 25:1–21 (NJB)

The sack of Jerusalem

In the ninth year of [King Zedekiah's] reign . . . Nebuchadnezzar king of
Babylon advanced on Jerusalem with his entire army . . . The city lay under
siege till the eleventh year of King Zedekiah . . . When famine was raging in
the city and there was no food for the populace, a breach was made in the
city wall. The king made his escape under cover of dark . . . The Chaldean
troops pursued the king and caught up with him in the Plains of Jericho,
where all his troops deserted. The Chaldeans captured the king and took
him to the king of Babylon at Riblah, who passed sentence on him. He had
Zedekiah's sons slaughtered before his eyes, then put out Zedekiah's
eyes and, loading him with chains, carried him off to Babylon . . . Neb-
uzaradan commander of the guard . . . entered Jerusalem. He burned
down the Temple . . . the royal palace and all the houses in Jerusalem. The
Chaldean troops . . . demolished the walls surrounding Jerusalem . . . They
broke up the bronze pillars from the Temple . . . the wheeled stands and the
bronze Sea . . . Thus Judah was deported from its country.

Zedekiah, the twenty-one-year-old un-
cle of the previous eighteen-year-old
King Jehoiachin, rebelled against the
King of Babylon after nine years of his
reign. The last thing he saw was his
own sons being slaughtered. We hear
no more of him, by contrast to his
nephew, who was released into
house-arrest after 37 years; doubtless
Zedekiah failed to survive his blind-
ing—he could hardly have been trea-
ted with antibiotics. To prevent any
further possibility of resistance, everything the Israelites had held sacred was
pillaged or destroyed.

The hope of Israel was now trans-
ferred to Babylon. Crippled at first with
guilt and despondency, they gradually
began to reflect on the lessons of the
disaster. With the help of the prophet
Ezekiel and the traditions of Jeremiah,
the tragedy became a source of growth:
their link to God was to rely no longer
on the institutions of Jerusalem but on
their own personal commitment, the
heart of stone was to be replaced by a
heart of flesh, capable of genuine,
personal love. A prophet in the tradition of Isaiah taught them even that
their suffering could be a source of
redemption for others.

Reflect
*Within them I will plant my Law,
writing it on their hearts. Then I shall be
their God and they will be my people.*

Jeremiah 31:33

Mark 2:27 (RSV)

Existing, not living

And he said to them, 'The sabbath was made for man, not man for the sabbath.'

One day very early in our marriage my wife took me to task. She said, 'We aren't living, we are only working—work, work, work.' She was right. I hadn't thought. Indeed I was being selfish. I wanted to succeed but you can't even succeed in life—let alone live—if there is nothing but work. So I did an about-turn. We expanded our annual ration of two weeks' summer holiday. We paid attention as well to the arts, to music, to nature and our garden. From then on we lived.

Sunday should be a safeguard against the tyranny of work. We should keep it slack. If we wear ourselves out driving all over the country, touring the country in powerful motorcars—or, for that matter, old crocks; if we sweat all day in the garden; if we use today to catch up on domestic chores, we have misused the day. A weekly day of rest is God-given. When God brought 'the children of Israel' out of the slavery of Egypt they must have danced with unbelievable joy with the news that for them one day in seven was to be a rest day. Slavery in Egypt or anywhere else had no room for rest days, no room for leisure 'to do one's own thing', to be with family and to laugh and sing. But it was God's plan for his people that these basics of human life should be possible and freedom granted to make it so.

Some people of course are forced to work on Sundays. They must take another day of rest and keep to it. And domestic work has to continue on Sundays. Could we not devise ways of lessening it? Christians cannot lay down rules how today is to be kept, certainly not for others and not for themselves either. But we need to pay attention to *the wisdom* of curtailing work on one day a week if we wish to live. All work is not living, it is existing, and some people's pleasure is so exhausting it looks uncommonly like work.

And for everyone's sake let us use the day to meet people and to talk, and I would add laugh and sing.

A prayer

Lord, thank you for our Sundays.
Give us the wisdom to guard them
as best we can.

DCF

Psalm 13 (RSV)

The ups and downs of faith

How long, O Lord? Wilt thou forget me for ever? How long wilt thou hide thy face from me? How long must I bear pain in my soul, and have sorrow in my heart all the day? How long shall my enemy be exalted over me? Consider and answer me, O Lord my God; lighten my eyes, lest I sleep the sleep of death; lest my enemy say, 'I have prevailed over him'; lest my foes rejoice because I am shaken. But I have trusted in thy steadfast love; my heart shall rejoice in thy salvation. I will sing to the Lord, because he has dealt bountifully with me.

Have you ever drifted down to the depths as far as your faith in God is concerned? Or are you one of those Christians who is always on top, never doubting, never despairing, never utterly cast down? Then don't bother with Psalm 13, it has nothing for you except perhaps pity for the wretched author. He seems to be in 'a bad way'. Who was he? David, perhaps, fleeing from King Saul bent on catching him and destroying him, and almost succeeding. Saul hated young David, seeing in him a dangerous rival to his throne. To read this Psalm, in the light of David's hair-raising escape from the tentacles of Saul, serves to bring home the agony of the Psalm. It underscores the ups and downs of our faith. Some of us are not always 'on top'. One day David thought he would by God's help escape Saul's deadly thrusts, the next day he wasn't sure. This is why I give this Psalm the title 'the ups and downs of faith'. Do you know what I mean?

What makes us sink down to the depths? Is it that man, that woman we dearly loved and for whom we prayed day by day but God let him/her die, the chemotherapy was awful? Is it the failure of that enterprise in which we put our heart and it became a write-off? Is it this physical pain, or that mental worry that won't go away whatever remedies we try? We stand peering through the windows of our souls and see nothing but smog.

But for the author of Psalm 13, whoever he was, the sun shone again. Read the last two verses again. Make them your own. I will. I have done it before, and I will do it again. Don't take the Psalter away from me. It is my life.

A prayer
Lord, you will not forget me, even me. You are my gracious Lord.

Psalm 14:1, 3–7 (RSV)

Widespread corruption

The fool says in his heart, 'There is no God.'... They have all gone astray, they are all alike corrupt; there is none that does good, no, not one. Have they no knowledge, all the evildoers who eat up my people as they eat bread, and do not call upon the Lord? There they shall be in great terror, for God is with the generation of the righteous. You would confound the plans of the poor, but the Lord is his refuge. O that deliverance for Israel would come out of Zion! When the Lord restores the fortunes of his people, Jacob shall rejoice, Israel shall be glad.

This psalm is about widespread corruption in the community, and it comes when there is a denial of God. The individual who boasts that 'there is no God' is a fool (the Hebrew word is *nabal*). Not a simpleton or an atheist. The fool here means the people who do not believe that moral principles operate at all in the world; we can all go on our way willy-nilly, there is nothing to stop us. This widespread foolishness develops into widespread corruption and one of the symptoms of this is the antagonism to God's people. In the twentieth century we have witnessed blatant and horrific examples of this on a vast scale in the persecution of the Jews.

Modern man does not take easily to this moral interpretaton of the corruption of communal life. In his view the causes can be readily traced to bad housing, class war, economic deprivation, poor education. These are the fields in which remedies are to be sought. The question of belief in God and recognition of the principles of living which such belief entails do not enter into the discussion. The *secular* state can be saved, indeed it can be made wholesome without God. But the Psalmist is very downright on all these views: he writes the word *NABAL* across them in capital letters.

Then he hits out: 'There they shall be in great terror, for God is with the generation of the righteous.' Are there not in our history books frightening records of the complete disintegration of nations that once seemed invincible, and not only in the distant past?

But the psalm ends on a higher note. 'When the Lord restores the fortunes of his people, Jacob shall rejoice, Israel shall be glad.'

A prayer

Lord, we pray for our nation. We pray for the Church in our nation. Give it grace and wisdom to keep alive faith in you as the Lord, the Lord of individual life and of communal life.

Psalm 15 (RSV)

Staying in touch with God

O Lord, who shall sojourn in thy tent? Who shall dwell on thy holy hill?
He who walks blamelessly, and does what is right, and speaks truth
from his heart; who does not slander with his tongue, and does no evil
to his friend, nor takes up a reproach against his neighbour; in whose
eyes a reprobate is despised, but who honours those who fear the
Lord; who swears to his own hurt and does not change; who does not
put out his money at interest, and does not take a bribe against the
innocent. He who does these things shall never be moved.

Psalm 14 painted a realistic picture of the mass of people totally devoid of belief in God and corrupt in their doings. Maybe this is too bleak a picture of the contemporary world, but Christian believers today are conscious of living in a godless environment. How then can we be in touch with God? This is the question Psalm 15 answers.

Maybe the situation is lit up for us if we think of David having written this Psalm when he had to flee from Jerusalem because it had been overtaken by hostile forces during Absalom's rebellion. David in his exile was cut off from his meeting place with God. How then could he be in touch with God?

Note that there is nothing about a location or a liturgy, important as those may be. The whole concentration is upon conduct and truth in the heart. This does not mean we can win or earn our way into the consciousness of the real presence of God close to us and caring for us. What it does mean is that

the deliberate liar, the twister in business and the shameless fornicator cannot hope to know anything of God's support in the ups and downs of daily life. He is cut off from communion with God, and what follows is a loss of God-consciousness.

We stay in touch with God if we consistently do what we know to be right and never twist the truth. There must be no slander or letting down of friends and no multiplication of reproaches against neighbours. The reprobate must be given no honour, only those who fear God. Promises must be kept, even if the keeping costs, and bribery is never to be countenanced specially to the disadvantge of the innocent.

To think about

Jesus put this psalm in a nutshell when he said, 'Blessed are the pure in heart, for they shall see God' (Matthew 5:8, RSV).

Psalm 16:1–2, 8–11 (RSV)

Hiding in God

Preserve me, O God, for in thee I take refuge. I say to the Lord, 'Thou art my Lord; I have no good apart from thee.' ... I keep the Lord always before me; because he is at my right hand, I shall not be moved. Therefore my heart is glad, and my soul rejoices; my body also dwells secure. For thou dost not give me up to Sheol, or let thy godly one see the Pit. Thou dost show me the path of life; in thy presence there is fulness of joy, in thy right hand are pleasures for evermore.

Turning from Psalms 13 and 14 and coming through Psalm 15 to Psalm 16 is like entering all of a sudden a lovely garden. You open the gate and stand there looking in amazement at the profusion of flowers that grasp your attention. And all this is more surprising because the author (David maybe) had been desperately ill, reckoning that he was about to die, as is clear from the last but one verse of the Psalm. But he crawled to God for refuge and did so trusting in God as the author of all goodness and loveliness.

And so we push on into the garden (as it were). There is not one word of complaint or questioning. The whole place is studded with gratitude, confidence about the present and the future and the expectation of pleasure still to come. The outreach of the Psalm is remarkable, so remarkable that Peter quoted it on the Day of Pentecost (see Acts 2:25–28) and Paul too (see Acts 13:35). And no wonder, for the Psalm intuitively stretches itself from a bed of sickness to the resurrection from the grave of Christ himself, with all its attendant hope of immortality for us all.

Can we rise to this Psalm? Can we enter this garden? In the modern world we are more likely to encounter a dismal wasteground, conspicuous for rank grasses and thistles. Complaints, resentments, dissatisfaction and rebellions abound. This is the landscape when people do not hide in God. There is nothing more important for a happy life than to hide there—believing in God, trusting him, and resting assured that he has good things prepared for us beyond our understanding, now and in the life to come beyond this life.

Prayer
Lord, lift me up to sing this Psalm today, at least in my heart and mind, if not in voice.

Psalm 17:1–2, 5, 8–13, 15 (RSV)

God hears the innocent

Hear a just cause, O Lord; attend to my cry! Give ear to my prayer from lips free of deceit! From thee let my vindication come! Let thy eyes see the right! ... My steps have held fast to thy paths, my feet have not slipped ... Keep me as the apple of the eye; hide me in the shadow of thy wings, from the wicked who despoil me, my deadly enemies who surround me. They close their hearts to pity; with their mouths they speak arrogantly. They track me down; now they surround me; they set their eyes to cast me to the ground. They are like a lion eager to tear, as a young lion lurking in ambush. Arise O Lord! confront them, overthrow them! ... As for me, I shall behold thy face in righteousness; when I awake, I shall be satisfied with beholding thy form.

Turn the page of the Psalter. You are no longer in the lovely garden of Psalm 16. The only similarity between these two Psalms is their final verses which both speak of the joy of ultimately being in the presence of God. Otherwise Psalm 17 depicts a clash of arms with raucous shouting and hideous threatenings, anything but a scene of serenity. To get the situation in focus read 1 Samuel 23:24–29. It tells of David and his men in the wilderness of Maon desperately seeking to escape King Saul, out to kill what he sees as a rival to his throne, which David certainly was not. Psalm 17 reflects the tension of this scarring scene.

Sometimes we find ourselves in alarming predicaments for which we can in no way be held guilty. Jealous self-seekers are out to 'get at' us. People resentful of our Christian faith, or who loathe the background from which we have come, or for any number of reasons. If we protest that we know nothing of such illogical hostilities then we must have been living on a desert island.

Let the Psalm tell us that we can take our hurt to God. He will hear us in our wilderness of Maon. He will justify our innocence and our rectitude—perhaps not granting us immediate deliverance but giving us the consciousness of his caring presence. One day the truth will out. That will be when we finally awake and meet God face to face.

Catch the mood of Psalm 17, and if our singing of it happens to be accompanied by an organ let the organist pull out all the strident stops, and then at the end alter the register entirely.

Prayer
Lord, preserve me from the bitter tongues that seek to do me hurt.

Psalm 18:16–19 (RSV)

A life rich in mercies

He reached from on high, he took me, he drew me out of many waters. He delivered me from my strong enemy, and from those who hated me; for they were too mighty for me. They came upon me in the day of my calamity; but the Lord was my stay. He brought me forth into a broad place; and delivered me, because he delighted in me.

The whole of this Psalm is set out in 2 Samuel 22 with this introduction: 'And David spoke to the Lord the words of this song on the day when the Lord delivered him from the hand of all his enemies, and from the hand of Saul.' The opening verses set the tone. 'The Lord is my rock, and my fortress, and my deliverer, my God, my rock, in whom I take refuge . . . I call upon the Lord, who is worthy to be praised, and I am saved from my enemies.' Primarily it fits the outcome of a battle, or some armed conflict when the fortunes of war swayed this way and that, but at last victory came, peace was restored. His theme is thanksgiving for a mighty deliverance. But we have deliverances in life other than in war when to sing this psalm is appropriate.

Do you know what it means to have been at death's door—but you came through? Have you laid awake at night wondering how to make ends meet—but you did? And that business which looked like collapsing, but it survived. All these are deliverances calling for songs of praise and thanksgiving in our life.

But there are many lesser mercies in our lives if we will only add them up. Could you sit down and write a list? I could. At the top of my list without a moment's hesitation I would put my wife, with whom I was blissfully happy for 54 years. I am sure God gave me her. She made my life. And my mother, a widow at 32. How can I be thankful enough to her for showing me how to surmount hardship? And that clergyman who put me in the way of becoming a biblical scholar. What about you? Could you make a list of God's mercies to you? Will you try? And when you have finished, read Psalm 18—out loud preferably. Then you might like to sing this verse of this hymn:

When all thy mercies, O my God,
My rising soul surveys,
Transported with the view, I'm lost
In wonder, love and praise.

J. Addison

Prayer
Thank you Lord for all your many mercies vouchsafed to me, even me.

1 Corinthians 12:4–7 (NIV)

Working together

There are different kinds of gifts, but the same Spirit. There are different kinds of service, but the same Lord. There are different kinds of working, but the same God works all of them in all men. Now to each one the manifestation of the Spirit is given for the common good.

Today there will be people all over the world meeting together in church to worship the living God who has given his gifts to his people.

Last year, when I took on two new readers in our church, we gained two brand new sets of gifts. However, our clergy team, which includes readers, became a new team, and that meant change. Our meetings had to take place sometimes on Saturdays because of one reader's work. It took time to get to know each other. But I must say that although it took effort to adjust, the changes were very good. Our care of people increased, our preaching became less pressurized and better prepared. We took on new projects and got things done which were previously left undone.

God knows that when his people work together using their gifts this is the most powerful instrument in his hand. Satan tries to isolate each Christian and render them ineffectual as we see in the Corinthian church. Paul sought to unite them in Christ.

I wrote a song once called 'The God machine'. It was based on a church I knew where the vicar had refused to carry on until the people really took on board this concept of every-member ministry. Two of the verses went like this:

The people all stared when the minister declared
That the services were cancelled due to lack of time.
They said, 'This is new but it really cannot do,
It's your job and you're just stepping out of line.'

'Something deep inside says you've got it very wrong Rev.,
You really ought to think what should be going on;
What kind of reformation have you caused by this sensation?
Your total congregation will be none.'

The truth was that his congregation grew.

I am convinced that this kind of working together is what God is commanding us to do. The increase in lay involvement in the Church has been a constant encouragement to me. Church today is about seeing different people doing different things, yet all worshipping the one Lord. May the common good be increased today.

GD

1 John

Although some scholars dispute the authorship of this epistle, we can reasonably follow the traditional view that it was written by John the apostle, with the author's claim to be a firsthand witness to Jesus—'the Word of Life ... which we have heard, which we have seen ... and our hands have touched' (1:1) ... 'We have seen and testify that that [he] has sent his Son to be the Saviour of the world' (4:14, NIV). It is a document that addresses a particular situation that had arisen, with the secession from the Church of a group of teachers who were the forerunners of the later heretics generally known as the 'gnostics' (from the Greek word *gnosis*, meaning knowledge). They claimed that their knowledge of God and of theology was superior to that of ordinary Christians. So the epistle, written to Church members—some of whom may have been wavering about leaving the Church to follow these supposedly 'superior' teachers—emphasizes '*that you may know*'. As lay Christians we can be confident about knowing God for ourselves.

And we can hold fast to the truth of Jesus, the incarnate Son of God, fully human and fully divine. The gnostics denied that Jesus was the Christ, the pre-existent Son of God, come in the flesh to provide salvation for men. Indeed, they claimed that they were sinless, disregarding any thought that their own lack of love might be sin. So another emphasis in the epistle is love. God is the source of all love, and we are repeatedly told to love one another, in phrases that are strongly reminiscent of John's record in his Gospel of Jesus with his disciples on the last night of his life.

Rosemary Green

1 John 1:1–4 (NIV)

The Word of life

That which was from the beginning, which we have heard, which we have seen with our eyes, which we have looked at and our hands have touched—this we proclaim concerning the Word of life. The life appeared; we have seen it and testify to it, and we proclaim to you the eternal life, which was with the Father and has appeared to us. We proclaim to you what we have seen and heard, so that you may have fellowship with us. And our fellowship is with the Father and with his Son, Jesus Christ. We write this to make our joy complete.

'In the beginning was the Word, and the Word was with God, and the Word was God' (John 1:1). That is how John starts his Gospel. He is very conscious of the eternity of Christ, the Word of life. But that eternal one has appeared, here and now. At the beginning of his Gospel he writes of John the Baptist as the one who 'came as a witness to testify concerning that light' (John 1:7). But now he emphasizes his own experience of the incarnate Word of life. 'We have seen, we have looked, we have touched.' He's *real*! And John wants his readers to share his conviction, not only intellectually but in experience, in the eternal Word who has come on earth. 'We have seen it and testify to it, and we proclaim to you.'

We can ask ourselves how far we identify with John. Do I share his certainty about the 'Word of life,' the eternal God who appeared on earth, who came in Jesus to bring us eternal life? We cannot share John's experience of seeing and touching Jesus on earth; but we can share his experience of meeting the living God. As Jesus said to Thomas, 'Blessed are those who have not seen and yet have believed' (John 20:29).

Do I share John's desire that others should come as well to know the living reality of Christ? He enjoyed fellowship with the Father and the Son; his joy would be complete when others came to share that fellowship.

A prayer

We thank you, Father, for the wonder of the Word of life. We pray that you will deepen our experience of him and our desire that others should know him too.
Amen.

1 John 1:5–7; 2:9–11 (NIV)

Walk in the light

This is the message we have heard from him and declare to you: God is light; in him there is no darkness at all. If we claim to have fellowship with him yet walk in the darkness, we lie and do not live by the truth. But if we walk in the light, as he is in the light, we have fellowship with one another, and the blood of Jesus, his Son, purifies us from all sin . . . Anyone who claims to be in the light but hates his brother is still in the darkness. Whoever loves his brother lives in the light, and there is nothing in him to make him stumble. But whoever hates his brother is in the darkness and walks around in the darkness; he does not know where he is going, because the darkness has blinded him.

Think of a hot summer's day: a clear sky, without a single cloud. The sun is so bright that we cannot look at it directly but as we walk outside we are fully aware of its light and heat. On such a day the shadows are sharp; there is strong contrast between the light and the dark. When we go indoors it is hard at first to see, because our eyes have become accustomed to the brightness of the light. That is a picture of the God who is light so bright that we cannot gaze straight at his dazzling holiness. But even though we cannot see him directly, he wants us to live in the purity of his sunshine, we who are Son-worshippers rather than sun-worshippers.

The biggest test, says John, of whether we are walking in the light or in the darkness is our relationship with other people. Love = light; hate = darkness. The contrast is as stark as the sharpness of the shadows on a sunny day. It would be good to take time as we pray today to think about the quality of our relationships with other people and our attitudes to them. Are there things we must put right? We can ask God to show us how to change things; maybe a letter of apology, a gift, an invitation, a prayer. Jesus told his disciples 'Love your enemies and pray for those who persecute you' (Matthew 5:44).

Pray

Pray the Lord's Prayer, slowly. See how many phrases link with today's reading.

1 John 1:8—2:2 (NIV)

Forgiveness assured

If we claim to be without sin, we deceive ourselves and the truth is not in us. If we confess our sins, he is faithful and just and will forgive us our sins and purify us from all unrighteousness. If we claim we have not sinned, we make him out to be a liar and his word has no place in our lives. My dear children, I write this to you so that you will not sin. But if anybody does sin, we have one who speaks to the Father in our defence—Jesus Christ, the Righteous One. He is the atoning sacrifice for our sins, and not only for ours but also for the sins of the whole world.

Can anyone claim to be perfect? Of course not! Yet how often we try to pull the wool over our own as well as other people's eyes. We make excuses for our wrongdoing or pass the blame on to someone else (Adam and Eve started that one! 'Her fault…', 'the serpent made me'). At other times we switch right the other way: 'I'm sorry, I'm sorry, it was all my fault.'

Evasion of blame and taking undue responsibility for wrong have a common root; our failure to take firm hold of the truth of the well-known words we have read today. 'If we confess our sins, he is faithful and just and will forgive our sins.' Our part is simple—'if we confess our sins'. We must acknowledge to God (and to ourselves) that we are in the wrong. His part is clear—'he will forgive our sins and purify us from all unrighteousness'. Our forgiveness depends on his character, 'faithful and just', and on Jesus who by his death on the cross 'is the atoning sacrifice for our sins'. I like the picture of Jesus as the counsel for the defence, standing before the Father who is a righteous, just judge.

We cannot earn our forgiveness in any way. Once forgiven, we must change our thinking and our behaviour. Jesus died 'for the sins of the whole world', but his death is effective only for those who choose to accept forgiveness on his terms.

A prayer

If I confess my sins, you are faithful and just and will forgive me my sins and purify me from all unrighteousness. Thank you, Lord.

1 John 2:24–27 (NIV)

Stay true to Christ

See that what you have heard from the beginning remains in you. If it does, you also will remain in the Son and in the Father. And this is what he promised us—even eternal life. I am writing these things to you about those who are trying to lead you astray. As for you, the anointing you received from him remains in you, and you do not need anyone to teach you. But as this anointing teaches you about all things and as that anointing is real, not counterfeit—just as it has taught you, remain in him.

These are difficult verses, from which we pick three strands to think about today:

God's promise John reminds us of a Jesus' promise to his followers of eternal life. That is a quality of life we can enjoy while we are still alive on earth; we do not have to wait till we die.

God's power Paul uses the word 'anoint' in 2 Corinthians 1:21–22: 'He anointed us, set his seal of ownership on us, and put his Spirit in our hearts as a deposit, guaranteeing what is to come.' He explains that God gave us his Spirit as a first instalment of his riches to come; as a seal to assure us that we really do belong to him; and as his anointing to set us apart for his service. John's 'anointing', too, alludes to the Holy Spirit of truth who teaches us about God.

God's protection When two hands are clasped together it is hard to say whether the left hand is in the right or the right hand is in the left. John says that 'the anointing you received from him remains in you'. God has given us his Spirit as a resident, to hold on to us; he will not remove that Spirit. But for our part we are to 'remain in him'; to keep in touch with him, not to withdraw ourselves from him, so that he and we stay clasped together. And John warns us about those who want to lead us astray. In the preceding verses he has been writing about the antichrist. There has been much speculation about who this antichrist is. Without knowing the answer, we can take to heart the warning that there are forces, both human and spiritual, who want to draw Christians away from following their Master.

A prayer
Father, I thank you for the foretaste of eternal life I can enjoy in this life through your Spirit. Please help me to draw on his power to stay true to you.

1 John 3:1–3 (NIV)

Children of God

How great is the love the Father has lavished on us, that we should be called the children of God! And that is what we are! The reason the world does not know us is that it did not know him. Dear friends, now are we the children of God, and what we will be has not yet been made known. But we know that, when he appears, we shall be like him, for we shall see him as he is. Everyone who has this hope in him purifies himself, just as he is pure.

Are you as thrilled as John was with the privilege of being a child of God? As I read the opening sentence I am caught afresh by John's wonder at God's love and his confidence in being a child of his heavenly Father. The Father has *lavished* his love on us. 'Lavished' is a word of extraordinary generosity. It is indeed incredibly generous of God that he should want to give us the privilege of being his children. We do not take it lightly; but we are meant to be as sure as John was. 'This is what we are!' This privilege has implications for the present and for the future.

For the present 'The world does not know us.' As children of God there is, inevitably, a measure of alienation from the world around us. Jesus, though human as well as divine, was rejected by his own people; misunderstood by his family, let down by his friends, crucified by his enemies. The world 'did not know him'.

For the future 'When he appears, we shall be like him.' I am reminded of Paul, writing to the Corinthians: 'Now we see but a poor reflection, as in a mirror.' Their mirrors, made of polished metal, did not give the clear reflection of modern glass. 'Then we shall see face to face' (1 Corinthians 13:12). We do not know exactly what Christ will be like when he comes in glory at his second coming; but we, the children of his Father, will be like him. What an incentive to pure, holy living now, as we seek to show people what God is like!

For meditation

How great is the love the Father has lavished on us, that we should be called the children of God.

1 John 3:11–15 (NIV)

Love one another

This is the message you heard from the beginning: We should love one another. Do not be like Cain, who belonged to the evil one and murdered his brother. And why did he murder him? Because his own actions were evil and his brother's were righteous. Do not be surprised, my brothers, if the world hates you. We know that we have passed from death to life, because we love our brothers. Anyone who does not love remains in death. Anyone who hates his brother is a murderer, and you know that no murderer has eternal life in him.

I am struck today by the black and white statements of this passage. It is a bit of a surprise; we might have expected John, the one who was known as an apostle of love, to be mellow and gentle in his old age. He affirms the fundamental message, 'We should love one another,' and then spells out some stark alternatives. Cain or Abel; evil or righteousness; hatred, murder and death, or love and eternal life. Love for our brothers may mean hatred from the world.

We live in an age when people do not, by and large, believe in absolutes; there is, apparently, no black and white truth, no defined standards of right and wrong. It reminds me of a verse in the Old Testament: 'In those days Israel had no king; everyone did as he saw fit' (Judges 21:25). When people do not acknowledge the King of kings the prevailing attitude becomes 'You can believe—or do—what seems right to you; I'll decide what is right for me.' Even the Church is undermined by

this climate of opinion that rates toleration above truth and puts self before others. But John tells us to 'love one another'. Love wants the best for another person. Love is strong, not weak. Love has high standards. Love is not afraid to stand up for the truth.

With these thoughts in mind, let us pray with David: 'Test me, O Lord, and try me, examine my heart and my mind; for your love is ever before me, and I walk continually in your truth' (Psalm 26:2–3).

1 Samuel 17:48–49 (NIV)

Let us pray

As the Philistine moved closer to attack him, David ran quickly towards the battle line to meet him. Reaching into his bag and taking out a stone, he slung it and struck the Philistine on the forehead. The stone sank into his forehead, and he fell face down on the ground.

To understand the significance of this familiar story we need to know a little of its history. The Philistines were a sea-going people from what is now Greece. They had settled in the Promised Land probably before the Israelites arrived. When God's people did eventually get there they found themselves in deep trouble.

The Philistines were subtle. They did not invade the country like some armies did. Rather they intermarried with the people of God corrupting them bit by bit. Of course the Israelites were also to blame for this, but by the time of Samson they had so compromised their faith there were few real followers of God left. Therefore God sent his judges. Samson took many of the ruling classes of the Philistines with him when he died at Gaza, but it was left for David to finish them off. So we have the story of David and Goliath.

I'm becoming increasingly aware of the compromises in my own life. There is a temptation for Christian people to think we've arrived. Not only that, but because we've arrived we can look back and have a little flirt with the world. We don't have a wild fling or revert to atheism, but neither are we wholeheartedly committed to God. I find this temptation strongest in prayer.

It's so easy not to pray. I'm tired or busy or forgetful and my prayer life dwindles to grace said at the table. And that's only because the children insist on it. Subtly, like a Philistine attack, I find I'm hardly praying at all. That's when it's time for a David and Goliath encounter. I have to face the problem head on, and it can seem to be about the same odds on me winning as it was for David to defeat Goliath.

However, often its a small thing like the stone that kills the giant. A throw-away comment which has helped me to recover my prayer life over the years was made by David Watson. He said he prayed for half an hour each day first thing in the morning, unless he had a really busy day . . . then he prayed for an hour!

GD

1 John 3:16–20 (NIV)

Love in action

This is how we know what love is: Jesus Christ laid down his life for us. And we ought to lay down our lives for our brothers. If anyone has material possessions and sees his brother in need but has no pity on him, how can the love of God be in him? Dear children, let us not love with words or tongue but with actions and in truth. This then is how we know that we belong to the truth, and how we set our hearts at rest in his presence whenever our hearts condemn us. For God is greater than our hearts, and he knows everything.

True love has its expression in lavish generosity. Love overflows in giving—our possessions, our time, ourselves, our lives. Last week our church calendar commemorated St Mary Magdalen. A story from the Gospels whose central figures are Jesus and (almost certainly) Mary makes a fitting commentary on John's words.

A week before his death Jesus was having dinner at the home of Simon, a Pharisee. A woman who was known as a prostitute brought a half-litre bottle of expensive perfume. She began to wet Jesus' feet with her tears; she poured the perfume over his head and his feet and wiped his feet with her long hair. Some of the spectators muttered 'Doesn't he know what sort of woman she is?' Judas and others complained—hypocritically—'What a waste! This perfume could have been sold for a year's wages and the money given to the poor.' But Jesus knew about the complaints. 'Stop bothering her! Her generosity is a mark of her love for me and her gratitude to me for forgiving her. She poured the perfume on my body to prepare it for burial.'

What a contrast between Mary's lavish giving and the tight-fisted Judas! Mean people often call the generosity of others a waste. But Mary gave unstintingly and was commended by Jesus, who knew her heart. It was a prelude to the unstinted giving of his own life. That is the standard he sets for us in dedication and in giving love that knows no boundaries.

To think about
He did this for you.
What can you do for him?

1 John 3:21–24 (NIV)

The heart of obedience

Dear friends, if our hearts do not condemn us, we have confidence before God and receive from him whatever we ask, because we obey his commands and do what pleases him. And this is his command: to believe in the name of his Son, Jesus Christ, and to love one another as he commanded us. Those who obey his commands live in him, and he in them. And this is how we know that he lives in us: We know it by the Spirit he gave us.

Command and obedience; obedience and confidence; loving relationships, a clear conscience and answered prayer; the indwelling Holy Spirit: they are all entwined. When we are trying to untangle a bundle of string it is often difficult to see where to start; it is the same with the 'tangle' of these verses. So instead of trying to write some logical explanatory thoughts we will use part of them to show how we can meditate on scripture.

'**Dear friends.**' How lovely that John could address as friends people he had never seen, with whom he was bound together by God's love. It reminds me that Jesus said to his disciples 'You are my friends if you do what I command' (John 15:14). 'Lord Jesus, thank you for that privilege.'

'**If our hearts do not condemn us.**' How good it is to have a clear conscience; how uncomfortable a guilty one! But I know that sometimes my conscience is confused. 'Holy Spirit, please educate my conscience by your holy truth, so that I

may respond aright to its whispers.'

'**We have confidence before God.**' It is wonderful to think that I can stand upright before a holy God, knowing that he forgives my wrong. 'God, I really do want to live in a way that pleases you. Thank you that your Spirit lives in me and helps me to obey you.'

'**We receive from him whatever we ask.**' If that is true it is a great responsibility, because I must try to find out what he wants me to ask for. That fits in with obeying his commands and pleasing him. 'Lord, please help me to walk hand in hand with you, so that my prayer and my lifestyle are tuned in with you.'

To think over

As you read the verses again and continue the meditation, what title would you like to give today's reading? I tried 'the heart of obedience', 'the keynote of assurance' and 'love and obey'. There could be others.

1 John 4:1–6 (NIV)

Test the spirits

Dear friends, do not believe every spirit, but test the spirits to see whether they are from God, because many false prophets have gone out into the world. This is how you can recognise the Spirit of God: Every spirit that acknowledges that Jesus Christ has come in the flesh is from God, but every spirit that does not acknowledge Jesus is not from God. This is the spirit of the antichrist, which you have heard is coming and even now is already in the world. You, dear children, are from God and have overcome them, because the one who is in you is greater than the one who is in the world. They are from the world and therefore speak from the viewpoint of the world, and the world listens to them. We are from God, and whoever knows God listens to us; but whoever is not from God does not listen to us. This is how we recognise the Spirit of truth and the spirit of falsehood.

The prevalent heresy of the day was an early form of gnosticism, a complex philosophy which so separated God from the created world, and the spiritual from the earthy, that Jesus was not perceived as truly human. Some gnostics thought that God's Spirit came upon him at his baptism but left before his passion; he was not both fully divine and fully human. Hence John's emphasis on the necessity to 'acknowledge that Jesus Christ has come in the flesh'. In the eyes of these 'false prophets' the bridge between God and man was broken at the human end. So John saw the gnostic teaching as the antithesis of the Christian faith: 'this is the spirit of the antichrist'.

'Test the spirits,' he says. In our late twentieth century we must test every teaching and every teacher by the standard of biblical orthodoxy and by the historic creeds that have been held by the Christian Church down generations. There are false prophets around today.

But John was not disheartened; neither need we be, because 'the one who is in you is greater than the one who is in the world'. We can ask the Spirit of truth, the Holy Spirit who dwells in us, to help us to recognize the spirit of falsehood, to ignore false teaching and to guide us into God's truth.

1 John 4:7–12 (NIV)

The heart of love

Dear friends, let us love one another, for love comes from God. Everyone who loves has been born of God and knows God. Whoever does not love does not know God, because God is love. This is how God showed his love among us: He sent his one and only Son into the world that we might live through him. This is love: not that we loved God, but that he loved us and sent his Son as an atoning sacrifice for our sins. Dear friends, since God so loved us, we also ought to love one another. No-one has ever seen God; but if we love each other, God lives in us and his love is made complete in us.

The Church Father Tertullian tells a story about John as an old man. He was taken into the Christian assembly in Ephesus and asked to preach. 'Love one another' he said—and stopped. They asked for more. 'Love one another.' 'Is that all?' they asked. 'Love one another,' repeated John; 'if that is done, it is enough.'

Love springs from the heart of God, who is love. Love is not merely a sentimental feeling, but a costly activity. As John said earlier in this letter, 'Let us not love with words or tongue but with actions and in truth' (1 John 3:18). It is not that our words should not express love, but words alone are hollow without solid evidence for their reality. There is no doubt about the way God showed his love for us: 'He sent his one and only Son into the world . . . as an atoning sacrifice for our sins.' That is the most costly gift love could give. No one coerced him; no one conscripted him. He gave because he loves us; he gave because his love wants us to live.

Over twenty years ago a plane crashed as it took off from the airport in Addis Ababa. My cousin stood by the door, helping others to escape from the flames—and died himself in the fire. Such stories give us glimpses of Jesus' love. David let go of his life so that other passengers might stay alive on earth. Jesus gave his life so that we may enjoy eternal life, in touch with God now and for eternity.

To think over
Do I really want to pray, 'Lord, please fill me to overflowing with your love'?

1 John 4:13–18 (NIV)

Christian assurance

We know that we live in him and he in us, because he has given us of his Spirit. And we have seen and testify that the Father has sent his Son to be the Saviour of the world. If anyone acknowledges that Jesus is the Son of God, God lives in him and he in God. And so we know and rely on the love God has for us. God is love. Whoever lives in love lives in God, and God in him. In this way, love is made complete among us so that we will have confidence on the day of judgment, because in this world we are like him. There is no fear in love . . . because fear has to do with punishment. The one who fears is not made perfect in love.

John displays a wonderful assurance about our relationship with God. These verses show us four strands about this assurance that he wants us to share.

'We know that we live in him and he in us.' Our lives are bound up with his when the Holy Spirit is living in us. It is the Spirit who assures us that we are truly God's children (Romans 8:15), the Spirit who is God's gift to us. So our assurance is not arrogance, because it is dependent on his generosity.

'We have seen and testify that the Father has sent his Son to be the Saviour of the world.' John knew Jesus as a person he lived with, whom he had seen crucified and risen again. Our experience of him can be as real; we do not meet him in the flesh but he comes alive to us through his Spirit. For us, as well as for John, the willingness to tell others—to testify—about that Saviour reinforces and en-hances our inner confidence about him.

'We know and rely on the love God has for us.' We can be sure of his love for us, not only because it is his very nature ('God is love') but because of the hard evidence of his love for us, that 'the Father has sent his Son to be the Saviour of the world'.

'We will have confidence on the day of judgment.' When we nestle into the Father's arms, sure that he loves us, fear melts—in particular, the fear of being punished by a harsh judge.

A prayer
Thank you, Father, that you want me to be sure about you.

1 John 5:11–16 (NIV)

Confidence in prayer

This is the testimony: God has given us eternal life, and this life is in his Son. He who has the Son has life; he who does not have the Son does not have life. I write these things to you who believe in the name of the Son of God so that you may know that you have eternal life. This is the confidence we have in approaching God: that if we ask anything according to his will, he hears us. And if we know that he hears us— whatever we ask—we know that we have what we asked of him. If anyone sees his brother commit a sin that does not lead to death, he should pray and God will give him life.

The theme of assurance continues: 'God has given us eternal life... He who has the Son has life... that you may know that you have eternal life.' Eternal life is God's gift; not wages to be earned, but a gift to be received when we 'believe in the name of the Son of God'. That belief is not mere mental assent, but a belief that is translated into active trust. I can stand beside a chair and say, 'I believe it is a good, safe chair'—and remain standing. Or I can act on that belief and sit down. That is a very simple illustration to show the difference between 'belief *about*' and belief *in*' the chair—or in the Son of God.

That quality of belief leads us to new confidence when we pray. No need for 'I wonder if he will listen to me' but 'we know that he hears'. This confidence, too, is not arrogance, because we can only be sure 'that we have what we asked of him' if 'we ask anything according to his will'. That means that we try to see things from God's point of view, not just our own. Our prayer will not be 'Give me' but 'Lord, what do *you* want?' We do not make demands of God or try to bend his will to ours, but we allow our will to be subordinated to his. 'Not my will, but yours be done' was Jesus' prayer in Gethsemane.

Yesterday we read that God 'has given us of his Spirit'. It is that Spirit, Paul tells us in Romans 8:26, who prays within us and through us when we are fumbling.

A prayer

'Thy kingdom come, thy will be done, on earth as it is in heaven.' Lord, please show me how to pray for your will, your kingdom to be fulfilled in me and in others.

Luke 7:44–48 (NRSV)

Little and great love

Turning towards the woman, [Jesus] said to Simon, 'Do you see this woman? I entered your house; you gave me no water for my feet, but she has bathed my feet with her tears and dried them with her hair. You gave me no kiss, but from the time I came in she has not stopped kissing my feet. You did not anoint my head with oil, but she has anointed my feet with ointment. Therefore, I tell you, her sins, which are many, have been forgiven; hence she has shown great love. But the one to whom little is forgiven, loves little.' Then he said to her, 'Your sins are forgiven.'

'The woman' referred to here is the one who stood behind Jesus as he dined in the house of Simon the Pharisee. While the respectable host looked on appalled, the woman—tactfully described by Luke as 'a sinner'—first washed the Lord's feet with her tears, then dried them with her hair, and finally anointed them with ointment.

Simon reckoned that if Jesus were a proper prophet he would have realized what sort of woman she was and told her to stop. Of course, he kept his thoughts to himself, but Jesus had this disconcerting way of seeming to know what people were thinking. He told Simon a little parable (vv. 41–42) about two people both forgiven their debts, one for a huge amount, the other for a trivial sum. Who would be the more grateful?

Simon knew the answer to that! The one who was forgiven most, he said. In response to his reply, Jesus drew his attention to the woman, who was presumably still standing behind him. Simon had not given Jesus even the normal courtesies of a host to his guest. But she had more than made up for it—washing his feet, drying and kissing them, and then anointing him with oil. Her love sprang from her sense of gratitude. Her sins, 'which were many', had been forgiven. Simon, whose sins were few (at least, in his estimation) had no sense of gratitude to Jesus at all. Her love overflowed in this wonderful gesture of worship. He was too busy criticizing and finding fault even to notice the significance of what she had done.

A reflection

When we understand how generous God's love is, and how undeserved, our worship, too, will be spontaneous and extravagant.

DW

Hebrews—— the eternal priest

The letter to the Hebrews is a bit of a mystery. No one knows who wrote it, though almost everyone who possibly could have has been suggested at one time or another, from Paul (the traditional, but certainly untrue, author) to the Virgin Mary.

In fact the letter may not even be a letter, as it lacks the normal greetings and other marks of a first-century letter. It may well be a sermon (so never complain about the length of modern sermons!) which was circulated like a letter.

We do not know to whom it was written, though its argument based on Jewish temple worship suggests that it was written to Jewish Christians (hence 'to the Hebrews').

The author is worried that his readers may lapse from their faith under either persecution or fierce Jewish argument (or both). So he sets out to show that while the Jewish way was ordained by God, it was only a precursor to the final salvation brought about by Christ.

The letter sees Jesus as a heavenly priest (indeed, the divinity of Christ is as explicit here as in John's Gospel) who offers himself as a final sacrifice for all sins. This sacrifice is final because it is the sacrifice of one who is eternal, and so it lasts forever. Look at Jesus, who he is, and all that he has done, says the author, and see what you lose if you lose him, and what you have if you cling to him.

In our short series of readings we can't cover the whole letter, but it is worth reading through if you can find the time. Some of it may seem difficult, but you'll find that there is much in this often underrated letter that is simply glorious.

Marcus Maxwell

Hebrews 1:1–4 (RSV)

Message of love

In many and various ways God spoke of old to our fathers by the prophets; but in these last days he has spoken to us by a Son, whom he appointed the heir of all things, through whom also he created the world. He reflects the glory of God and bears the very stamp of his nature, upholding the universe by his word of power. When he had made purification for sins, he sat down at the right hand of the Majesty on high, having become as much superior to angels as the name he has obtained is more excellent than theirs.

Hebrews doesn't let you in gently. In the first paragraph there's enough material to form the basis for a dozen text books of theology and prayer and meditation for a lifetime.

We are told that Jesus Christ, the Son of God, is the agent God used to create the world. We are told that he still is the one who holds the universe in being. He bears the nature of God—he is, then, in some sense, God himself. So creation and salvation are tied together in Christ—all that God does, he does through the Son, and his acts are part of the one great act.

We are told that Christ's status is not just his by nature, but has been earned, through his saving work of wiping out sin, and his kingship is based not just on might, but through effort.

All this and more will crop up again in Hebrews, but none of it can compare with the really stupendous message—that this Creator, redeemer, being who is greater than the angels, the one who bears the nature of God, this Son of God, has come as a messenger to us. People may have seen angels, they may have heard the words of prophets, but in Jesus God's creating power has come himself to speak to us.

The message Jesus brings is, like the messenger, far greater than the words of the prophets. Jesus, of course, spoke and taught, but far beyond that he was the message itself. In all he said and did, and above all in his death and resurrection, he played out God's message for us: that we are loved.

Pray

Father, thank you for such love that comes to us in Jesus, that goes to the cross for our sins, and conquers death that we may live. Make me in every way a hearer of your message, and help me to share it with others.

Hebrews 2:1-4 (RSV)

The most important thing

Therefore we must pay the closer attention to what we have heard, lest we drift away from it. For if the message declared by angels was valid and every transgression or disobedience received a just retribution, how shall we escape if we neglect such a great salvation? It was declared at first by the Lord, and it was attested to us by those who heard him, while God also bore witness by signs and wonders and various miracles and by gifts of the Holy Spirit distributed according to his own will.

If Jesus really is God's message to us, and the gift of salvation he brings really does open up a new life and a new relationship with God, it must be the most precious thing we have. Not only that, but to turn our backs on it must be the greatest disaster we could face.

Writing to Christians who are tempted to let go of their faith, the writer makes a simple point, but one which is easily forgotten. If Christianity is true, it can only be the most important thing in the world.

Yet, it is so easy to see only the outward trappings of faith, and to place them on the same level as (or lower than) many other aspects of life. We probably all know the Sunday morning debate: to go to church, or to cut the lawn, visit relatives, wash the car, do the housework. The simple action of going to church may seem on the same level as these other things, but what it represents is not. It is about the relationship of love and abundant life which we have with God.

How, asks the writer, can his readers think this way, when the message of love which is Jesus has been relayed to them by his disciples, and they have seen God's mighty acts? At times, we too need to look back over our lives and remind ourselves of just what our faith has meant to us, how we have seen God at work in our lives, and just what it is that he offers, and we are too often tempted to ignore.

Think
How important is God in your life?

Hebrews 2:5–9 (RSV)

Human destiny

For it was not to angels that God subjected the world to come, of which we are speaking. It has been testified somewhere, 'What is man that thou art mindful of him, or the son of man, that thou carest for him? Thou didst make him for a little while lower than the angels, thou hast crowned him with glory and honour, putting everything in subjection under his feet.' Now in putting everything in subjection to him, he left nothing outside his control. As it is, we do not yet see everything in subjection to him. But we see Jesus, who for a little while was made lower than the angels, crowned with glory and honour because of the suffering of death, so that by the grace of God he might taste death for every one.

By now it is fairly clear what the writer's argument is: see how great Jesus is, what wonderful things he has done for you, and see therefore how foolish it is to turn away from him just because discipleship has become difficult.

We have been shown the divine nature of Jesus, sent as God's message to us, and the folly of rejecting his salvation. Now we are reminded of the possibilities of human destiny.

Psalm 8 sees human beings as the crown of God's creation, set by their Creator to rule over all the world. Yet that is not how things really are. We struggle in an often hostile world, against the forces of nature and human evil. Man in general, then, is not triumphant. But one man is—Jesus.

We do not yet see him fully in control, but as we look at the cross, we see the triumph of the man Jesus; a triumph over sin and death, and the opening of a new relationship with God.

With that triumph, a new humanity is made possible. As we are joined with Christ in the family of God we at last are able to discover our true human destiny. Not to be lost forever in weakness and failure, nor to be at the mercy of a hostile world, but to be transformed into the glorious children of God.

It is a destiny which lies in the future, but is already beginning to be realized through the power of the Holy Spirit. This is what Jesus has done for us—opened the way to full humanity. Who, then, could settle for less?

Hebrews 2:14–18 (RSV)

Man of two worlds

Since therefore the children share in flesh and blood, he himself likewise partook of the same nature, that through death he might destroy him who has the power of death, that is, the devil, and deliver those who through fear of death were subject to lifelong bondage. For surely it is not with angels that he is concerned but with the descendants of Abraham. Therefore he had to be made like his brethren in every respect, so that he might become a merciful and faithful high priest in the service of God, to make expiation for the sins of the people. For because he himself has suffered and been tempted, he is able to help those who are tempted.

Long ago, one of the great medieval theologians, St Anselm, wrote a book called *Cur Deus Homo* ('Why the God-Man?') in which he attempted to demonstrate from first principles why the incarnation was necessary. His argument wasn't that far different from this one in Hebrews.

The idea is of a divide between humans and God. The divide is caused by human sin, which means that it has to be put right from the human side. Yet the only power which can put things right lies with God. What is needed, then, is some way of bringing the power of God into the human side of the equation, to deal with the problems of sin and death which cause the divide. The way to do it is for God to become human.

Hebrews tells us that Jesus had to become like us in order to represent us to God as the perfect high priest. We tend to find the priest language a bit obscure, because it is tied up with the system of sacrificial worship which ended centuries ago. Yet the idea remains a good one. Jesus stands with a foot in both worlds, God and man, forming a bridge between humans and God. When we put our faith in him, the bridge is open, and we can cross into a new relationship with God.

That's why we so often use the prayer formula 'through Jesus Christ'. The man of two worlds forms the connection between the two, and becomes the way into heaven for us.

Pray

Thank you, Lord, for being the way to salvation and eternal life, for being one with us, and for bringing us hope and victory.

Hebrews 3:1-6 (RSV)

Family pride

Therefore, holy brethren, who share in a heavenly call, consider Jesus, the apostle and high priest of our confession. He was faithful to him who appointed him, just as Moses also was faithful in God's house. Yet Jesus has been counted worthy of as much more glory than Moses as the builder of a house has more honour than the house. (For every house is built by some one, but the builder of all things is God.) Now Moses was faithful in all God's house as a servant, to testify to the things that were to be spoken later, but Christ was faithful over God's house as a son. And we are his house if we hold fast our confidence and pride in our hope.

The Jewish Christians to whom Hebrews was written came from a tradition of pride. They were proud of their history and of their founders, especially Moses. They were proud of being God's people. And the writer has no quarrel with that. Yet in the face of their threatened defection from the faith he asks where their pride is now.

If Moses was someone to be proud of, how much more was Jesus, who outshines Moses in every way. Moses was the servant of God (and none greater!) but Jesus is the Son of God, and what he has achieved is greater still. So instead of letting opposition turn them aside from faith, it should deepen their pride.

For us, this may seem even stranger than talk of high priests and sacrifice. We have been taught to think of pride as a sin (one of the seven deadly). And even more, we are hardly ever proud of belonging to the Christian faith, perhaps because we are often reminded (rightly) of the shortcomings of the Church, both past and present.

Yet the writer doesn't point to the Church, but to Jesus. Consider Jesus and all he has done. We belong now to his 'house', his family. Family pride is something we do understand. Our families may not often be up to much, but they are ours. Woe betide the one who offends our family!

We belong to Jesus. That's nothing to be ashamed of. That's something to make us hold up our heads. Never mind what I am like, I belong to the greatest family in the world!

Think

We need never be ashamed of our faith, for Jesus is our pride and joy.

Hebrews 3:7–11, 16–19 (RSV)

Holding fast to God

Therefore, as the Holy Spirit says, 'Today, when you hear his voice, do not harden your hearts as in the rebellion, on the day of testing in the wilderness, where your fathers put me to the test and saw my works for forty years. Therefore I was provoked with that generation, and said, "They always go astray in their hearts; they have not known my ways." As I swore in my wrath, "They shall never enter my rest." ' . . . Who were they that heard and yet were rebellious? Was it not all those who left Egypt under the leadership of Moses? And with whom was he provoked forty years? Was it not with those who sinned, whose bodies fell in the wilderness? And to whom did he swear that they should not enter his rest, but to those who were disobedient? So we see that they were unable to enter because of unbelief.

After Moses brought the Israelites out of Egypt they wandered in the desert for forty years. Not because it was a forty-year journey to Canaan, but because God was forging a people of faith. The generation that left Egypt demonstrated its lack of real trust in God time and again. Only their children knew God well enough to stick to him once they were in the Promised Land.

The fate of that first generation became proverbial for those who distrust and rebel against God. So Psalm 95, which our writer quotes, looks back to those events and makes them a call to faith. And Hebrews also uses the same warning for those who are in danger of turning away from God.

When I was a young Christian (literally and figuratively) a big issue was the question of the permanence of salvation. If someone who had been a believer fell away, did they lose their hope of eternal life? The answer is probably more complex than the simple yes or no that student debates demanded. It is also rather pointlessly theoretical. The real issue is whether we decide to remain with God. Whether or not we may ultimately be saved, what matters is how we are with God today.

Those who reject their faith may or may not finally end up in heaven. But they lose the peace, the joy and the hope that God wants us to have here and now as we grow in faith and service. And he loses helpers and lovers whom he wants here and now.

Think

What has tempted you to lose heart and faith? What has kept you going?

137

Philippians 1:3–6 (NRSV)

I've started, so I'll finish

I thank my God every time I remember you, constantly praying with joy in every one of my prayers for all of you, because of your sharing in the gospel from the first day until now. I am confident of this, that the one who began a good work among you will bring it to completion by the day of Jesus Christ.

Magnus Magnusson, of *Mastermind* fame, has made a very odd statement into a catch-phrase: 'I've started, so I'll finish.' But it's not a bad motto for life. There is something very sad about incomplete things, and something very satisfying about finishing a job properly. Jesus could say to his Father at the end of his life, 'I have finished the work you gave me to do.' It had been hard and painful, and ended on a cross, but he had done it.

Here Paul is assuring the young church at Philippi that God—not the apostle—would complete the good work he had begun among them, in his own time ('by the day of Jesus Christ').

What was true for Philippi is true for St Philip's, if you see what I mean! We may feel that many tasks are incomplete. Our Sunday school class doesn't seem to respond. Confirmation candidates drop away. Numbers aren't what they were. But what God has started he will finish. It is his work, not ours.

And what is true of churches is true of individuals. We may have children who were baptized and brought up in the faith, but now seem far from it. But if God began a work, if even a 'mustard seed' of faith was planted, then God will complete what he began. What he has begun he will bring to 'completion', to his own satisfaction, like a master craftsman. There are no loose ends with God!

A reflection

Help us, Lord, to trust that what you have begun you will complete in your own good time: in the Church, in those we pray for, and in ourselves. Amen.

DW

Hebrews 4:3–7 (RSV)

Rest

For we who have believed [are entering] that rest, as he has said, 'As I swore in my wrath, "They shall never enter my rest,"' although his works were finished from the foundation of the world. For he has somewhere spoken of the seventh day in this way, 'And God rested on the seventh day from all his works.' And again in this place he said, 'They shall never enter my rest.' Since therefore it remains for some to enter it, and those who formerly received the good news failed to enter because of disobedience, again he sets a certain day, 'Today,' saying through David so long afterward, in the words already quoted, 'Today, when you hear his voice, do not harden your hearts.'

After quoting the warning of Psalm 95, our writer gives a complex interpretation of the threat 'they shall never enter my rest'. Briefly, he sees this as a reference to the 'rest' of God after finishing creation. But this rest was not a simple end of work, instead it is a state of blessed satisfaction which we might call 'heaven' and which God offers to share with his people. Those who reject God fail to enter the rest, but the offer still remains open.

There is a certain day on which the offer can be taken up, but don't mark it on your calendar, because it is 'Today'. And this is the real point. Those who have faith in God begin a process of entering that rest. We have not yet arrived (we're not in heaven) but we are on the way.

So every day, each 'today', becomes a day of decision, a day of continuing to enter the bliss and joy of God.

In some churches you will still find 'testimony meetings', where the members are given an opportunity to declare what God has done for them. Usually this is the story of how they came to faith. But here we are reminded that the first finding of faith is not the whole story. Each day is a day of 'conversion', a day in which we decide to live for and with God.

Today, when you hear his voice, say, 'Yes.'

Pray

Thank you, Father, for calling me. Let my response be always the same: Yes.

Hebrews 4:14–16 (RSV)

One of us

Since then we have a great high priest who has passed through the heavens, Jesus, the Son of God, let us hold fast our confession. For we have not a high priest who is unable to sympathize with our weaknesses, but one who in every respect has been tempted as we are, yet without sin. Let us then with confidence draw near to the throne of grace, that we may receive mercy and find grace to help in time of need.

If the writer has seemed to cajole and threaten a little, with his appeals to what Jesus has done and his reminder of the fate of those who abandon God, he makes up for it with this well-known passage.

The one who represents us to God is not a distant and awesome figure, but a human being like us. Like us, Jesus knows what it means to be tempted, and understands human weakness from the inside. To say that he did not sin doesn't lessen his understanding, but provides hope that he has help to offer. (No one buys hair tonic from a bald man!)

And in fact, Jesus does have help to offer, for his sinlessness was not a result of an inability to sin (or he couldn't have been tempted) but a result of his total reliance on God. So the temptation the original readers felt, to give up on Christianity, is not insurmountable. If they come to God for his grace and mercy, they will receive it.

Grace and mercy are two of the best words in the Bible. Mercy, because it holds out hope to those who do sin that God will bring forgiveness and a new start. Grace, the undeserved giving of God, because it holds out hope that we will receive the strength we need to keep going.

Christians never have to give up, because there is always grace and always mercy.

Reflect

On the times you have needed God's forgiveness, and God's strength. How have they come to you? And do you look for them now?

Hebrews 5:1–5 (RSV)

Pattern for ministry

For every high priest chosen from among men is appointed to act on behalf of men in relation to God, to offer gifts and sacrifices for sins. He can deal gently with the ignorant and wayward, since he himself is beset with weakness. Because of this he is bound to offer sacrifice for his own sins as well as for those of the people. And one does not take the honour upon himself, but he is called by God, just as Aaron was. So also Christ did not exalt himself to be made a high priest, but was appointed by him who said to him, 'Thou art my Son, today I have begotten thee.'

Yesterday's theme continues as the writer considers the (idealized) qualifications of a high priest. The priest was appointed to represent the people to God, and to offer sacrifices on their behalf. This is what Jesus does, presenting his own death as a sacrifice for us. He stands as the mediator between God and humanity.

The priest is also there to offer teaching and guidance, and this too Jesus does, as our guide and leader (an image that comes later in Hebrews).

The main qualification is being able to sympathize with human weakness. This, as we have seen, Jesus can do. But it is the qualification for all high priests; and I don't think it is much of a stretch to say that that applies to all people in a priestly role.

Whatever our view of Christian ordination or priesthood, it is clear that there are those in the Church who are called to give teaching and guidance. In fact, all of us have found ourselves exercising such a 'priestly' role from time to time.

The key to success in that ministry is weakness. It is not superior strength that encourages, but shared suffering and temptation. In our sharing with others we should never be ashamed to own up to weakness or to limitations. In our clergy, we should never look for superhuman talents or spirituality, but for fellow pilgrims who are willing to share their experience as our teachers and leaders and to pray for us out of a deep understanding of human frailty.

Reflect

How have other people's experiences of weakness been a help to you? Has your understanding of weakness or failure been a help to others, or a source of deeper prayer?

Hebrews 5:7–10 (RSV)

Perfection

In the days of his flesh, Jesus offered up prayers and supplications, with loud cries and tears, to him who was able to save him from death, and he was heard for his godly fear. Although he was a Son, he learned obedience through what he suffered; and being made perfect he became the source of eternal salvation to all who obey him, being designated by God a high priest after the order of Melchizedek.

If Jesus was sinless, how could he be 'made perfect'? On the face of it, it seems a contradiction, but we can get at the answer, and at the meaning of our passage, by asking another question: when Jesus was a little boy, was he sinless? And if so, was he ever naughty?

The answer is that he (presumably) was sinless, but that he almost certainly was naughty. Because being naughty is part of being a child, and part of growing up. We learn about the rules by which we are expected to live, and about the nature of tolerance and love, by testing them as we grow.

And so we have different standards for people of different ages. Acceptable behaviour in a six-year-old is out of place in a teenager, and teenage behaviour in a fifty-year-old is a sign of serious problems. To be human is to grow and to develop, and perfection in a human being cannot be a serene state of perpetual bliss, but is a movement and a dynamic process.

And so Jesus was made perfect by growing through his life in an appro-priate way. And he grew up to the point where he faced his Father's refusal to save his life, obeyed his Father's will, and in his death bought salvation for us.

At the same time he provides a pattern for us. Whether or not perfection is possible for us, growth is. We, too, are called to develop in obedience to God, awareness of his will and love for him and for others. Perhaps above all, we can learn as Jesus did, that prayer which is not granted is none the less answered.

Think

Are you still growing? Or have you become content with things as they are?

Hebrews 5:11—6:3 (RSV)

Growing and learning

About this we have much to say which is hard to explain, since you have become dull of hearing. For though by this time you ought to be teachers, you need some one to teach you again the first principles of God's word. You need milk, not solid food; for every one who lives on milk is unskilled in the word of righteousness, for he is a child. But solid food is for the mature, for those who have their faculties trained by practice to distinguish good from evil. Therefore let us leave the elementary doctrine of Christ and go on to maturity, not laying again a foundation of repentance from dead works and of faith toward God, with instruction about ablutions, the laying on of hands, the resurrection of the dead, and eternal judgment. And this we will do if God permits.

'I'm interested in practical faith, not doctrine.' 'I have a simple faith, Vicar, I don't like it too complicated.' How often we hear words like these, especially when we're advertising Bible studies or confirmation courses and the like. There seems for many modern Christians to be a feeling that using our minds to learn about the faith is somehow an unspiritual exercise, totally unrelated to our prayer, worship and service.

Or do we fear deeper understanding will challenge our faith, and make us look again at our walk with God?

Either way, our writer ties together an understanding of faith with spiritual maturity and discernment. You ought to be teachers by now, he says, not still struggling with basic doctrines. And he's right. If we cannot explain our faith, how can we share it with others? If we do not understand what we say we believe, how can we really believe it? If we have not explored the Bible's teaching about God and Jesus, how can we recognize what is God's will?

The simple fact is that understanding and faith go hand in hand. Wrestling with our understanding and wrestling in prayer are closely related, and spiritual growth follows in the footsteps of mature learning.

I suspect the devil knows that too. Which is why teaching the Christian faith is one of the few widely recognized sins. (It's called ramming religion down people's throats.) In a Bible study I was once accused by a stalwart church member of trying to indoctrinate her. I was. But putting doctrine into people is what we should be about.

Think

Do you separate faith and understanding, and, if so, why?

Hebrews 6:4–8 (RSV)

Stern warning

For it is impossible to restore again to repentance those who have once been enlightened, who have tasted the heavenly gift, and have become partakers of the Holy Spirit, and have tasted the goodness of the word of God and the powers of the age to come, if they then commit apostasy, since they crucify the Son of God on their own account and hold him up to contempt. For land which has drunk the rain that often falls upon it, and brings forth vegetation useful to those for whose sake it is cultivated, receives a blessing from God. But if it bears thorns and thistles, it is worthless and near to being cursed; its end is to be burned.

In our last two readings, the author has been stressing the need to keep growing, to keep moving on in the faith. Development is the normal process of human life. We do not stand still, and we do not go backwards.

From this he draws a terrifying conclusion. If we attempt to go backwards, to turn away from God, having truly encountered him, we can never return again, for to turn away from Christ is to make a mockery of him and effectively stand with his crucifiers.

Of course, on the face of it, he is wrong. Many of us will know those who have lost their way, and their faith, for a while, but have returned home again. Yet there is a deep truth here. Those who turn their backs on God, and do so deliberately, are turning their backs on the giver of forgiveness. How then can they possibly repent?

Apostasy, remember, is not quite the same as overwhelming doubt. It is a deliberate denial of the truth of a belief once firmly held and the rejection of an experience once cherished. I suspect that it is not the same, even, as denying the faith out of fear, for then there is shame and regret. Deliberate apostasy is more an act of pride.

I know an ex-clergyman who is now a great opponent of Christianity. I gain the impression that he is angry with God, whom he almost wants to hurt. If I am right, I don't think he can be brought to repentance because he doesn't want to repent, and doesn't want forgiveness. But if once he does feel that need, I am equally sure he will find it waiting for him. It is we who deny God, never he who denies us.

Pray

For all who, for whatever reason, deliberately reject God, and so lose themselves.

Matthew 5:14–16 (NRSV)

Shining as reflectors

[Jesus said:] 'You are the light of the world. A city built on a hill cannot be hid. No one after lighting a lamp puts it under a bushel basket, but on the lampstand, and it gives light to all in the house. In the same way, let your light shine before others, so that they may see your good works and give glory to your Father in heaven.'

This is part of the passage in the Sermon on the Mount where Jesus talks about his followers and their influence on the world around them. They are to be 'salt' (v. 13), preserving the world from corruption. And they are to be lights, shining the presence of God into their community—they are to give light to 'all in the house', like a well-placed lamp on its stand. Their salt will be useless if it loses its taste. Their light will be ineffective if it's hidden under a 'bushel bag'—presumably a bag big enough to carry a bushel of goods, and big enough not only to cover but to extinguish any household lamp.

The message to his followers is clear: 'You are the light of the world.' But surely Jesus is the 'light of the world' (John 8:12)? Yes, that's exactly the point! They, and we, are not so much lights as reflectors—moons to his sun. What we shine into the world is not our goodness ('your good works'), but his.

And whatever credit we get for it is his, not ours. So we 'let our lights shine'—in the lives we live and the love we show—but the glory is not ours, but 'our Father in heaven's'. That is why it is not enough simply to 'live the life' (though that is primary and essential). We must also 'name the Name'. People need to know that whatever good they see in us is not ours, but comes from God. We are reflectors, not self-generating lamps!

A reflection

Give me grace, Lord, to shine as a light in the world, reflecting the love of Jesus. And give me grace to make sure that the glory for it goes to you! Amen.

DW

Hebrews 6:9–12 (RSV)

Kingdom come

Though we speak thus, yet in your case, beloved, we feel sure of better things that belong to salvation. For God is not so unjust as to overlook your work and the love which you showed for his sake in serving the saints, as you still do. And we desire each one of you to show the same earnestness in realizing the full assurance of hope until the end, so that you may not be sluggish, but imitators of those who through faith and patience inherit the promises.

Despite the dire warning against apostasy, the author of Hebrews does not really believe that such a fate lies in store for his readers. They may be tempted to lapse from the faith, but they have a lot going for them—their love. Whatever their failings, they have not lost the love of God and each other which should be the defining mark of Christians.

In fact, this is the only part of the letter in which any real degree of warmth shows through. Perhaps fear for his readers has lent a degree of harshness to the message, but here those who are marked by love are reminded that they too are loved, and it the love of the writer which makes him so afraid for those he loves.

Yet they still need more. Ahead of them lies the hope of eternal life, promised by God. Here and now they must live in that hope. 'Realizing the assurance of hope' does not simply mean clinging on to the vision of what is to come, but making that vision real in the here and now.

The fact that heaven lies ahead, that the kingdom of God will win out, should colour our lives in the present. It is because Christians have been given a hope for the future that they have a different perspective on the present.

We are called to live our lives by the values and ideals of the kingdom that is to come. As the 'Hebrews' found in practice, a sign of that kingdom is love. But another sign is faith. If God is Lord of our future, he can also be trusted here, where his lordship so often seems in doubt.

Because of the hope of heaven, Christians now are called to be pointers to heaven, to offer to the world, through word and deed, an alternative which looks to God and his values.

Think

How do our lives, and that of our church, bear witness to the kingdom of God?

Hebrews 6:13–20 (RSV)

Promises

For when God made a promise to Abraham, since he had no one greater by whom to swear, he swore by himself . . . Men indeed swear by a greater than themselves, and in all their disputes an oath is final for confirmation. So when God desired to show more convincingly to the heirs of the promise the unchangeable character of his purpose, he interposed with an oath, so that through two unchangeable things, in which it is impossible that God should prove false, we who have fled for refuge might have strong encouragement to seize the hope set before us. We have this as a sure and steadfast anchor of the soul, a hope that enters into the inner shrine behind the curtain, where Jesus has gone as a forerunner on our behalf, having become a high priest for ever after the order of Melchizedek.

Swearing these days is something we do when we hit our thumb with a hammer. In the ancient world, it was a much more serious thing. A promise or contract was verified by calling on a god to stand as guarantor of the promise. And it was expected that the god would act to keep the promisor to his word.

God, says the author, has sworn a similar oath to be true to his promise to Abraham and all his people. Not that God could swear by another person, but since God is the one everyone else swears by, we know he can be trusted. All this is a way of saying that when God says he will do something, there is no question about it. He will do it. God has promised salvation to his people, and we can actually see that these are not empty words, for Jesus has already paved the way for us.

Just as the high priest in Jerusalem was permitted into the holiest part of the temple on behalf of the whole people, so Jesus has gone ahead of us to prepare a place for us.

Our hope, then, is based on these two things: that Jesus has paved the way for us, and that he acts now as our go-between with God. This means that our faith is not based on our own efforts, or our own feelings, but on what Jesus has done for us.

Meditate

On all that Jesus has done, and on the way to God he makes available to us.

Hebrews 7:1–3 (RSV)

Mel who?

For this Melchizedek, king of Salem, priest of the Most High God, met Abraham returning from the slaughter of the kings and blessed him; and to him Abraham apportioned a tenth part of everything. He is first, by translation of his name, king of righteousness, and then he is also king of Salem, that is, king of peace. He is without father or mother or genealogy, and has neither beginning of days nor end of life, but resembling the Son of God he continues a priest for ever.

The meeting of Abraham with Melchizedek is a rather obscure piece of the story of Abraham, but it made a great impression on later generations. Abraham, the man of God, received the mysterious king's blessing, and gave him a tithe of his possessions. We are not told of Melchizedek's birth or death or ancestry. And so he becomes for our writer an image of Christ, who has no beginning nor end, and is greater even than Abraham.

The points being made about Jesus are clear: first, he is the one who blesses us, and to whom, in return, we offer our giving and indeed our selves. This is always the pattern with God. He comes first to us, and then we respond. It's a strange fact that despite the Church's teaching for nearly 2,000 years, most folk today would say that Christians believe that if they are good they will go to heaven. Nothing could be further from the truth. We believe that God has blessed us with the promise of heaven, and so we try to be good, to worship him and serve him.

Secondly, Jesus (once again!) is our priest. He stands on our behalf, to bring us to God. He is always there to receive our prayer, to guide and help us, and to bring us renewal and forgiveness. No wonder that yesterday's reading described him as an anchor for the soul. When all else fails, we still have Jesus, and nothing can remove him.

Pray

Thank you, Father, that we can come to you through Jesus and always be sure of a welcome, for in him you have first come to us, accepting us as we are, and making us your own.

Hebrews 8:1–5 (RSV)

Shadowlands

Now the point in what we are saying is this: we have such a high priest, one who is seated at the right hand of the throne of the Majesty in heaven, a minister in the sanctuary and the true tent which is set up not by man but by the Lord. For every high priest is appointed to offer gifts and sacrifices; hence it is necessary for this priest also to have something to offer. Now if he were on earth, he would not be a priest at all, since there are priests who offer gifts according to the law. They serve a copy and shadow of the heavenly sanctuary; for when Moses was about to erect the tent, he was instructed by God, saying, 'See that you make everything according to the pattern which was shown you on the mountain.'

We can begin to skip a bit now, for the letter goes on at length to stress the points we have already seen in looking at Jesus as the heavenly high priest. A new idea comes in today's reading, though, that things on earth are 'shadows' of things in heaven.

The notion is borrowed from the Greek philosopher, Plato, whose theories were widely held in the first century. Plato taught that everything on earth gains its essential nature by sharing some quality with an 'idea' or ideal example of that thing. So that a chair is a chair because it shares certain qualities with the perfect 'heavenly' chair. All that may sound rather strange to us, but it is ideal for conveying a spiritual truth.

According to our writer, the tent of worship which Moses erected, and on which the Jerusalem temple was based, was patterned on the heavenly temple in which Jesus offers himself as a sacrifice on our behalf.

The truth of this for us focuses on worship. The worship we offer is patterned on the worship of heaven. Here worship is a pale shadow of the joy and exuberant wonder of heaven. Yet the pattern is the same. As Jesus offers himself wholeheartedly to God, so we offer ourselves in our worship. As Jesus receives the gift of salvation for us, so we receive God's grace. And there are moments (all too rare) when the reality of heaven really seems to break into our worship, and the sense of joining 'with angels and archangels and all the company of heaven' becomes a living reality.

To remember when you worship

This is only a shadow of the real thing, but the solid, genuine article may well appear when you least expect it.

Hebrews 9:11–14 (RSV)

Saved for what?

But when Christ appeared as a high priest of the good things that have come, then through the greater and more perfect tent (not made with hands, that is, not of this creation) he entered once for all into the Holy Place, taking not the blood of goats and calves but his own blood, thus securing an eternal redemption. For if the sprinkling of defiled persons with the blood of goats and bulls and with the ashes of a heifer sanctifies for the purification of the flesh, how much more shall the blood of Christ, who through the eternal Spirit offered himself without blemish to God, purify your conscience from dead works to serve the living God.

More than once I've heard someone jokingly say, 'God wants to save me? What does he want to save me for?'

What indeed? Of course, the joke is based on 'save' as in saving stamps, rather than as in rescue. But the question is a fair one. What does God do with us once he has us? Hebrews is much concerned with how Jesus saves us, using the imagery of priesthood and sacrifice. But here we are told what comes next. We are saved ('purified') 'to serve the living God'.

That service is seen in Hebrews in an almost liturgical sense; the service which is worship and self-offering. Has it ever seemed strange to you that we call our acts of worship 'services'? Yet worship is service (the word 'liturgy' comes from a Greek word meaning something like 'public service'). It is service because God has made us to love him and obey him. When we worship we are doing something which he wills, and in which he rejoices. So it is just as much service as more obviously active tasks (and as we have seen, it is much more permanent—eternal, even).

Another service is to love, for in loving we share God's love with those around us. Already we have seen the first readers of Hebrews praised for their love. In that, they were certainly servants of God.

Another service is to share our faith with others. Earlier in the letter, we read that we should be teachers. Not in the sense that all must be leaders of study groups or preachers, but that all Christians, by their witness to Christ, teach the faith to those around them.

So this is what we are saved for: to serve God in worship, in love and in proclamation of the faith.

Think
Do you do what you are saved for?

Hebrews 9:24–28 (RSV)

Sacrifice

Christ has entered, not into a sanctuary made with hands, a copy of the true one, but into heaven itself, now to appear in the presence of God on our behalf. Nor was it to offer himself repeatedly, as the high priest enters the Holy Place yearly with blood not his own; for then he would have had to suffer repeatedly since the foundation of the world. But as it is, he has appeared once for all at the end of the age to put away sin by the sacrifice of himself. And just as it is appointed for men to die once, and after that comes judgment, so Christ, having been offered once to bear the sins of many, will appear a second time, not to deal with sin but to save those who are eagerly waiting for him.

In our brief look through Hebrews, we have time and again been told that Jesus' death was a sacrifice. Yet can it be meaningful to use such terms today?

In one sense, the answer must be no. For Christians and non-Christians alike, the idea of sacrificial worship is at best a quaint idea from the past, and at worst a rather revolting and meaningless act.

At the same time, though, the language of sacrifice has entered our thinking to such an extent that we hardly notice it. We talk of sacrificing pieces in chess, of sacrificing time, money, health in pursuit of some desired goal.

We probably all know of someone who has sacrificed career or marriage or happiness in order to care for an elderly parent or handicapped child. We read often of someone who has risked or lost their life to save another. And on this level, the notion of Jesus as a sacrifice speaks very loudly.

In coming to live among us, in dying for us, Jesus has given up the power of Godhead, and life itself, in order to win our well-being for all eternity. Jesus stands as the great model for all who sacrifice themselves, and tells us that at the very heart of existence, in the core of creation's meaning, is the idea of sacrificial love.

Sacrifice is still one of the most powerful images of what Jesus and his death stand for. It does not give us a 'mechanism' of salvation; we are not told exactly how it 'works'. But then, how could we be? It is a wonder beyond comprehension. We can only gaze in awe at the sacrifice, and receive what it gains for us.

Jeremiah 20:7–9 (NRSV)

Fire in his bones

O Lord, you have enticed me, and I was enticed; you have over-powered me, and you have prevailed. I have become a laughingstock all day long; everyone mocks me. For whenever I speak, I must cry out, I must shout 'Violence and destruction!' For the word of the Lord has become for me a reproach and derision all day long. If I say, 'I will not mention him, or speak any more in his name,' then within me there is something like a burning fire shut up in my bones; I am weary with holding it in, and I cannot.

The Oxford Dictionary defines a 'jeremiah' as a 'dismal prophet', which—as you can see in this passage—is very unfair on the original Jeremiah. He was a reluctant prophet, called by God to warn the people of the southern kingdom, Judah, that unless they repented they would follow the people of the northern kingdom of Israel into captivity. It wasn't his message, and as we read here, he didn't like it. But it was the truth, and real prophets tell the truth. It was a long while before his prophecy was fulfilled—long enough for the people to give him a bad time, and turn to the more congenial messages of the false prophets, who cried 'Peace, peace!' where there was no peace.

It's a vivid and challenging picture of the person who stands for God's truth, even when it is unpopular and unwelcome. Notice, Jeremiah didn't enjoy it—though one suspects some prophets of hell-fire and damnation secretly do! He spoke what he believed with all his heart to be the truth. The fact that it brought him ridicule and mocking (v. 7), reproach and derision (v. 8) and desperate inner conflict and pain (v. 9) could not deter him. Nor should they deter us.

He describes God's word as 'like a burning fire in my bones' which he simply could not hold in any longer. Like Paul's cry, 'Woe to me, if I do not preach the gospel!' he knew the deep inner compulsion of the true messenger. We could do with more of it!

A reflection

Lord God, help me not to shrink back from witnessing to your truth, whatever the cost.

DW

Judges 16:19–22 (NIV)

Samson

[Delilah] called a man to shave off the seven braids of his hair, and so began to subdue him. And his strength left him. Then she called, 'Samson, the Philistines are upon you!' He awoke from his sleep and thought, 'I'll go out as before and shake myself free.' But he did not know that the Lord had left him. Then the Philistines seized him, gouged out his eyes and took him down to Gaza. Binding him with bronze shackles, they set him to grinding in the prison. But the hair on his head began to grow again after it had been shaved.

Fortunately the Bible is full of good news for those who have failed. I've never been as powerful or as strong or as resourceful as Samson, but what I do have in common with him is the experience of giving in when the pressure becomes unbearable. This can apply at work or at home or in any situation where 'getting things right' requires consistent care and attention.

It can be so dispiriting. It's many years since I gave up smoking (I used to smoke sixty cigarettes a day and I enjoyed every single one), but I can still remember the attempts I made to stop when I was in my late twenties and early thirties. For some reason I got the idea into my head that God was going to 'get me' if I didn't stop smoking, so I was always worrying about it. Sometimes I'd manage to last for a week, a month, or even a couple of months, but then the pressure would become unbearable, especially if some other worry had become more dominant, and I'd fail again and feel a miserable failure. I didn't understand God at all in those days, so each time I was pretty sure I'd lose my salvation at the very least. Why would he want to be bothered with someone who had let the enemy batter him into submission?

The fact was, though, that after each of these failures, and there were many, my hair began to grow again, as it were, just like Samson's. Some kind of divinely natural healing process restored both my belief that I was valued, and my intention to please God, and, in the end, I did give up smoking, although it was sheer agony for about six months.

Please don't think, by the way, that I'm getting at you if you're a smoker. God deals with each of us differently, and in my case, it was my experience that when people went on at me about giving up, there was only one thing I wanted to do—go and have a fag!

Prayer

Father, sometimes we give in under pressure, and it feels as if we will never be quite as close to you ever again. Restore the strength of our trust in you, Lord, and keep us close to you in future.

Daniel 2:26, 29–30 (NIV)

Daniel

The king asked Daniel (also called Belteshazzar), 'Are you able to tell me what I saw in my dream and interpret it?' Daniel replied, 'No wise man, enchanter, magician or diviner can explain to the king the mystery he has asked about, but there is a God in heaven who reveals mysteries. He has shown King Nebuchadnezzar what will happen in days to come. Your dream and the visions that passed through your mind as you lay on your bed are these: As you were lying there, O king, your mind turned to things to come, and the revealer of mysteries showed you what is going to happen. As for me, this mystery has been revealed to me, not because I have greater wisdom than other living men, but so that you, O king, may know the interpretation and that you may understand what went through your mind.'

Do read the whole of Daniel as if it was a novel, if you have not done so before. It's a marvellous piece of story-telling (no, I'm not saying it didn't happen, just that it's a good read), and a very clear picture of the way in which God operates through a life that is genuinely dedicated to him. The impressive thing about Daniel, in all his dealings with the Babylonian kings, is his refusal to extract any personal glory from the situations in which God has given him special knowledge or protection. In this particular case he is at great pains to make it clear that it is God, not himself, who is the ultimate revealer of mysteries, and that his qualifications for passing on the wisdom of God do not include any extra or unusual wisdom of his own. The consistent purity of motivation shared by Daniel and his three famous friends, makes them very strong. No one can truly damage the most important part of you if your first priority is to serve God.

We could do with a few Daniels in Church leadership today. It's so easy, when involved in spiritual ministry, to put on a bit of a self-advertising show, instead of simply passing on whatever God has told you to. The great sadness about this is that, for both Christians and non-Christians, the glorious sanity of God can be obscured by quite unnecessarily dramatic and bizarre role-playing on the part of those who have power over others. I hope and pray that the Church may be entering a new phase in this country, one that will see God speaking and working more clearly and more powerfully than ever before. I just hope that, when this happens, we'll be like Daniel, and get out of the way.

Thought

When the time comes to face the lions, relationship is going to be worth more than religion.

Joshua 5:13–15 (NIV)

Joshua

Now when Joshua was near Jericho, he looked up and saw a man standing in front of him with a drawn sword in his hand. Joshua went up to him and asked, 'Are you for us or for our enemies?' 'Neither,' he replied, 'but as commander of the army of the Lord I have now come.' Then Joshua fell face down to the ground in reverence, and asked him, 'What message does my Lord have for his servant?' The commander of the Lord's army replied, 'Take off your sandals, for the place where you are standing is holy.'

Thirty days after the death of Moses, Joshua, the new leader of the Israelites, was filled with the spirit of wisdom, which was just as well because he was going to need it. He must, in any case, have learned a great deal from his old master, described by the writer of Deuteronomy as the greatest prophet ever seen in Israel. Perhaps, in particular, he might have learned the folly of attempting to out-guess God. And here's another good example.

Thank goodness he didn't rush bloodthirstily at this armed man and try to cut him to pieces. He might have done, mightn't he? Buoyed up by the reproach of Egypt having been lifted, and the experiences that year of eating from the produce of Canaan for the first time instead of being sustained by manna, Joshua must have been feeling pretty good. What an interesting answer the commander of the army of the Lord gave to his question. Why did he say 'neither'? Why didn't he say, 'Well, I'm for you of course'?

Perhaps Joshua needed a little reminder about who was actually in charge. Perhaps his question should have been: 'Are you for the Lord or for his enemies?' Perhaps it was essential that, like Moses, he should be humbled on holy ground, especially as the whole Jericho extravaganza was about to take place.

We can very easily find ourselves swept away by the excitement of doing things for God. But woe betide us if we lose touch with the roots of our excitement and begin to see the world in terms of those who are for *us* and those who are against *us*. We are not in charge of our own lives, and if we go around tackling our personal Jerichos without reference to the real commander, the walls are very unlikely to come down.

Prayer
Meet us on holy ground, Lord, and remind us that you are in charge.

Zephaniah 3:18–20 (NIV)

Zephaniah

'The sorrows for the appointed feasts I will remove from you; they are a burden and a reproach to you. At that time I will deal with all who oppressed you; I will rescue the lame and gather those who have been scattered. I will give them praise and honour in every land where they were put to shame. At that time I will gather you; at that time I will bring you home. I will give you honour and praise among all the peoples of the earth when I restore your fortunes before your very eyes.'

I used to think I was the only person in England who'd ever read Zephaniah, but there must be a few others, mustn't there?

I can't remember if I've written about this passage in these notes before. It's a very significant piece as far as I'm concerned, and I really hope it might be helpful to you as well. It became especially important to me when I was in the middle of a stress illness (yes, that's right—the same tedious old stress illness that I always seem to be bleating on about). I had arrived at just about the lowest point it was possible to reach, and I really could not see how I would ever achieve spiritual, emotional, or financial stability again. I had abdicated from work, church and proper family commitment to such an extent that I wasn't able to even look at the problems that I was facing.

God used a number of things to haul me out of that state, including friends, family and some specific experiences of his closeness, but this short passage from dear old Zeph, if I

may call him that, was a small but key influence on my gradual return to normal lunacy. Don't ask me why some Bible verses stand out so vividly—I don't know how the Holy Spirit does it. What I do know is that the compassion and love expressed in these promises from God to his people became promises from him to me, tickets for a Liverpool-Manchester match in my inside pocket. In particular, I loved the final line, as expressed in this translation. I sensed a delight in the heart of God about his plans magically to transform my fortunes.

I do hope that those of you who are in the same position as I was will also feel that delight, and tuck the promises away carefully so that you can take them out from time to time and draw a little strength from them.

Prayer

Father, thank you for illuminating your words when it's necessary. Be with all those who have reached the end of their tether. Do some magic in their lives.

Genesis 33:1–4 (NIV)

Jacob and Esau

Jacob looked up and there was Esau, coming with his four hundred men; so he . . . put the maidservants and their children in front . . . He himself went on ahead and bowed down to the ground seven times as he approached his brother. But Esau ran to meet Jacob and embraced him; he threw his arms around his neck and kissed him. And they wept.

The power of these Old Testament stories is quite extraordinary, isn't it? I've just read the section that leads up to this historic meeting, and when the two brothers wept, so did I. Do the same and you'll see why I ended up all gooey. Jacob was so *worried* that Esau's head would still be full of the dastardly trick played on him by his brother all those years ago when Jacob (famously 'a smooth man') got the blessing from Isaac instead of Esau. Jacob was quite brave though, wasn't he? He was determined to encounter his brother whatever the consequences, and I suppose that shows how much he'd changed since the days when he so easily outsmarted the slightly bovine Esau.

During the years that they'd been apart Jacob had met an even sharper con-man than himself—Laban, his father-in-law—and he'd wrestled with God and was still limping as a result. This was not the same Jacob, and perhaps he should have realized that Esau would also have moved on from the resentment of the past.

Reconciliation is often like this. Our fear of rejection or conflict can separate us for years from people whom we once loved, would still love if we felt sure that reconciliation was possible. When we do actually take the plunge, it is often the case that both parties experience a tremendous joy on rediscovering a relationship that was always greater and more valuable than the reason for its fracturing.

Jacob's courage (despite his fear) didn't just result in peace between the two brothers, important though that was. His return to the country of his birth was an essential step in the history and destiny of what was to be known as the Israelite nation.

My making-up with Auntie Ada over what she said about our Billy thirty-five years ago, when she'd had one sherry too many after Sunday dinner, might not seem to be in quite the same league as Jacob and Esau, but who knows? Shall we try?

Prayer

Father, some of us have some peacemaking to do. It's frightening. Give us courage and determination, and an awareness that it's part of your plan for the future.

Genesis 45:4–8 (NIV)

Joseph

Joseph said . . . 'I am your brother Joseph, the one you sold into Egypt! . . . Do not be angry with yourselves for selling me here, because it was to save lives that God sent me ahead of you. For two years now there has been famine in the land . . . But God sent me ahead of you to preserve for you a remnant on earth and to save your lives by a great deliverance. So then, it was not you who sent me here, but God. He made me . . . ruler of all Egypt.'

This is one of the greatest Old Testament stories of all, but do you think Joseph got this bit right? I mean—obviously he was bowled over by seeing his brothers again, but was it really God who did it all? Was it God who initiated the idea of slinging Joseph into a cistern, and then somehow silently persuaded the brothers to sell him to traders, just so that Isaac and his family wouldn't starve years later? And what about the fact that these incidents led eventually to the suppression and oppression of the Jewish people by an Egyptian nation that grew to hate them? Is that what God was planning all along?

If that was the case, then shouldn't we feel free to do whatever we feel like doing, however harmful it may be to others, confident in the knowledge that God is really behind our actions, and that therefore we can put the responsibility onto him? An attractive way to look at things, perhaps.

Forget it! Seductive though that approach to Christian living may be, we have been privileged to hear the words and sense the personality and presence of Jesus, who came to show us what God is actually like. These Old Testament accounts are marvellously entertaining and profoundly instructive on many levels (Jesus himself quoted them often in support of his own teaching), but we would do well to temper both the unacceptable and the attractive aspects of this section of our Bible with the knowledge we have gained through the revelation of God in Christ.

Jesus made it clear that we are responsible for our own actions. He also showed us the depth of the love of God for us by going to the cross, and he did that for the very good reason that not a single one of us will be able to make our actions match the holiness of God.

The Bible—all of it—is full of God, but Jesus *was* God.

Prayer

Father, we thank you for the passion and drama and humour and wisdom of the Old Testament. We wrestle with some of the nasty bits, but you've let them be there, so thank you for those as well (by faith!). Most of all we thank you for Jesus, who came to reveal you and save us.

New Daylight BRF © 1996

The Bible Reading Fellowship
Peter's Way, Sandy Lane West, Oxford, OX4 5HG
ISBN 0 7459 3237 1

Distributed in Australia by:
Albatross Books Pty Ltd, PO Box 320, Sutherland,
NSW 2232

Distributed in New Zealand by:
Scripture Union Wholesale, PO Box 760, Wellington

Distributed in South Africa by:
Struik Book Distributors, PO Box 193, Maitland 7405

Distributed in the USA by
The Evangelical Education Society of the Protestant
Episcopal Church, 2300 Ninth Street South, Suite
301, Arlington, VA 22204

The Bible Reading Fellowship
P O Box M, Winter Park, Florida 32790

Publications distributed to more than 60 countries

Cover photograph: Jon Arnold

Printed in Denmark

75TH ANNIVERSARY SERVICE

To mark BRF's 75th Anniversary, there will be a Service of Thanksgiving and Rededication at 12 noon on Thursday 30 January 1997 in Westminster Abbey, London.

This will be an occasion for us to give thanks for 75 years of BRF ministry in many countries around the world, to remember all those who have so faithfully served the Fellowship both on the staff and in the churches over the years, to celebrate all that God is doing in and through BRF today, and to rededicate ourselves for the tasks and challenges that lie ahead.

We hope very much that many of you, the readers of *New Daylight*, will be able to join on us on this important occasion, and we extend a very warm invitation to you all.

Admission to the service will be by ticket only, and we have approximately 1,500 tickets available for our readers and subscribers. If you would like to apply for tickets (applications limited to two tickets per person) please complete the form below and send it to:

75TH ANNIVERSARY SERVICE TICKET DEPT
BIBLE READING FELLOWSHIP
PETER'S WAY
SANDY LANE WEST
OXFORD OX4 5HG

Ticket applications will be processed strictly on a first come, first served basis. We will advise you if your application arrives after all the tickets have been allocated. If you do not hear from us, you may assume that tickets have been reserved for you, and these will be despatched to you approximately two weeks before the Service takes place.

(PLEASE PRINT)

Name: . . . .

Address: . . . .

. . . .

. . . . Postcode: . . . .

Please send me ONE/TWO* tickets for the BRF 75th Anniversary Service in Westminster Abbey on 30 January 1997.

*delete as appropriate